OSPREY AIRCRAFT OF THE ACES • 65

Beaufighter Aces of World War 2

SERIES EDITOR: TONY HOLMES

OSPREY AIRCRAFT OF THE ACES • 65

Beaufighter Aces of World War 2

Andrew Thomas

OSPREY
PUBLISHING

Front cover
On the evening of 15 February 1941, Flt Lt John Cunningham and his navigator Sgt Jimmy Rawnsley of No 604 Sqn took off from Middle Wallop in their Beaufighter IF R2101/NG-R. They were to establish a patrol line south of Lulworth, which they flew at 15,000 ft under the control of 'Starlight' Ground Control Intercept (GCI) station. Soon after arriving in the area, their controller advised them that an intruder was inbound at 12,000 ft. Cunningham descended 1000 ft below the enemy bomber to silhouette it above them. As well as checking their Air Intercept (AI) radar, the crew scanned ahead visually. Rawnsley spotted another aircraft high to port. He later wrote;

'John brought the Beau wheeling round on its wingtip. The enemy was a tiny black speck, still miles away but incredibly distinct against the opal curtain of light. It must have been 1000 ft higher than we were, and it was coming our way fast, growing bigger and more like a Heinkel every second. I turned to look down-light, trying to see how far he could see in our direction. It was certainly very murky looking that way, with the sea and the sky blending into a dull grey haze.

'The Heinkel was soon high overhead, and John turned in order to keep beneath it. Apparently they had not seen us, and continued serenely on their way. John held his position below them, keeping watch through the roof panel. For a very long ten minutes we continued in company, and all the time it was getting darker. But now, all too plainly for my liking, the Dorset coast was showing up. Perhaps the German skipper thought the same thing. The Heinkel went into a slow turn to the right. Steadily, John went into a shadowing turn, glancing up and down from the bomber to his instruments.'

The Heinkel orbited over Lyme Bay until it was fully dark, before heading north once more. Cunningham maintained station, then, opening the throttles, closed on the bomber until it was above them. Sgt Rawnsley continued;

'The Heinkel sank slowly into our sights. I waited for the "hot tomatoes" to come streaming back at us when our guns started their giant pounding. For the first few seconds nothing at all seemed to happen. Then, through the choking haze of smoke from the guns, I saw a flash of hits on the starboard engine as John shifted his aim.'

But at that point the ammunition ran out as the bomber entered a slow descent. From the navigator's position, Rawnsley feverishly began changing the 60-lb ammunition drums. By then Cunningham had lost sight of his target, but the GCI station vectored them in again as the Heinkel headed west along the coast. Cunningham set off in pursuit, although the target's height made the AI radar unreadable. At 3000 ft the Beaufighter crew saw incendiaries explode on the ground some distance ahead as they were jettisoned. Soon afterwards a flash of flame marked where the Heinkel hit the ground between Poole and Totnes. This was Cunningham's third kill, and the first of many scored with Rawnsley. It was also the first of ten, plus a probable and two damaged, that they would claim in R2101. Their victim was He 111P-2 Wk-Nr 2911 of 7./KG 27, which crashed at Higher Luscombe Farm, Harberton. Lt Eberhard Beckmann and his crew were killed.

This painting by Mark Postlethwaite shows Cunningham and Rawnsley stalking their prey over the Dorset coast in the last streaks of daylight before attacking after dark

First published in 2005 by Osprey Publishing
Midland House, West Way, Botley, Oxford OX2 0PH, UK
443 Park Avenue South, New York, NY 10016, USA
Email: info@ospreypublishing.com

ISBN 1 84176 846 4

Edited by Tony Holmes and Bruce Hales-Dutton
Page design by Tony Truscott
Cover Artwork by Mark Postlethwaite
Aircraft Profiles by John Weal and Scale Drawings by Mark Styling
Index by Alan Thatcher
Origination by PPS Grasmere Ltd, Leeds, UK
Printed in China through Bookbuilders

05 06 07 08 09   10 9 8 7 6 5 4 3 2 1

ACKNOWLEDGEMENTS
The author wishes to record his gratitude to the following former Beaufighter pilots and navigators who have given of their time in answering queries and presenting accounts of their actions for inclusion in this volume: F W Baldwin, Wg Cdr A D McN Boyd DSO DFC, Sqn Ldr D H Brocklehurst DFC, F Cassidy, the late AVM E D Crew CB DSO DFC, D H Greaves DFC, Gp Capt R C Haine OBE DFC, Wg Cdr R F Martin DFC, Wg Cdr G H Melville-Jackson DFC and Gp Capt J A O'Neill DFC. The author is also grateful to the many friends and fellow enthusiasts, too numerous to mention, who have generously given support to bring this volume to fruition.

CONTENTS

CHAPTER ONE

THE OPENING ROUND 6

CHAPTER TWO

COUNTERING THE *BLITZ* 9

CHAPTER THREE

BAEDEKER AND BISCAY 21

CHAPTER FOUR

AROUND THE MEDITERRANEAN 46

CHAPTER FIVE

IN TROPICAL SKIES 69

CHAPTER SIX

THE LAST BATTLES 81

APPENDICES 84
COLOUR PLATES COMMENTARY 91
INDEX 96

THE OPENING ROUND

'I was vectored out 170 (degrees) and back 350 onto an enemy aircraft, and I sighted the enemy at about 16,000 ft. I observed the enemy flying slightly to my north side ahead of me at a distance of 400 yards. I opened fire at 200 yards, firing approximately 200 rounds in two bursts. I gave a third burst at 70 yards but the cannon failed to fire. My AI (Air Intercept) operator observed the enemy aircraft dive steeply into cloud. The enemy aircraft returned no fire. This aircraft was definitely a Do 17 or 215 as I noticed the humped effect above the forward end of the fuselage (where the aerial is) and its high wing, as well as the twin rudders.'

So wrote Sgt Arthur Hodgkinson of No 219 Sqn on the night of 25 October 1940, having just claimed the first of his 11 victories. It was also the first enemy aircraft to be shot down by the pugnacious Bristol Beaufighter, a powerful and deadly new twin-engined fighter developed by the Bristol Aeroplane Company in response to a perceived need for a long-range fighter. Based on the company's Beaufort torpedo bomber then currently under construction, the Beaufighter was large and powerfully-armed, equipped with four Hispano 20 mm cannon and six Browning 0.303-in machine guns.

First flown in July 1939, the Beaufighter's pace of development was such that just over a year later, with the Battle of Britain at its height, the first production aircraft were delivered to operational units – R2056 went to No 25 Sqn, R2072 to No 29 Sqn, R2070 to No 219 Sqn, R2065 to No 600 Sqn and R2073 to No 604 Sqn. All were designated as nightfighter squadrons and all flew converted Blenheim light bombers fitted with gun packs. Some were also fitted with AI radar. The Beaufighters of the initial batch were fitted with the cannon only, but also had the AI Mk IV radar with the characteristic 'bow and arrow' nose and wing blade aerials.

One of the first Beaufighter Is delivered to an operational squadron was R2069, which went to No 25 Sqn at Debden. Initially flown in factory-applied day fighter camouflage, the aircraft were soon painted black, but this example was still wearing these colours when flown by future ace Flg Off Mike Herrick the following spring (*RAFM*)

Operations began on 17 September when No 29 Sqn's CO, Wg Cdr S C Widdows, with Plt Off Watson as radar operator, flew an uneventful patrol in R2072. The first unit declared operational, however, was 'B' Flight of No 219 Sqn after it had moved to Redhill. The other units, too, worked up intensively as the Beaufighter's capability was desperately needed with the Luftwaffe turning increasingly to night attacks against Britain's seemingly defenceless cities. The frustration is evident from the comments of future ace Flg Off Johnny Topham;

'My time with No 219 Sqn was eventful, particularly in respect of the development of a nightfighter system, the whole of which had to function satisfactorily before, in early 1941, interception successes began to happen at night – too late, regretfully, for us to have any effect on the 1940 bomber raids on London and elsewhere. We were at Redhill during this period, but could do no more than watch the frightful devastation.'

He was airborne on the night of 25 October when Hodgkinson, with Sgt Benn, in R2097 claimed the aircraft's significant 'first'. It acted as a powerful morale-booster. The Beaufighter had a great impact on its pilots, many of whom would gain considerable success flying it. One was pre-war Auxiliary Flt Lt Roderick Chisholm of No 604 Sqn, who said;

'One day at the end of October 1940, the first Beaufighter arrived at Middle Wallop. On the ground it was an ominous and rather unwieldy looking aircraft, with its outsize undercarriage and propellers and small wings, but in the air it looked just right. It had an improved type of radar and four cannon but, most important of all, it had a cockpit out of which the pilot could see well. If there were sufficient external guides – a skyline or moonlit ground – it was easy enough to fly steadily, as in daylight. But if these aids were absent, the night very dark and visibility poor, instrument flying in the early Beaufighter called for unceasing and most exacting concentration.'

It was the combination of the Beaufighter's performance and armament, allied to the development of ground radar control to position the nightfighter close enough to enable it to pick up targets on its own AI radar for the final attack, that eventually began to help counter the Luftwaffe's night *Blitz* on Britain. One of the first radar contacts of an enemy aircraft came in the early hours of 18 November. Flg Off 'Bob' Braham of No 29 Sqn, who later became the most successful Beaufighter ace, gained a fleeting contact. But the first success came the following

The leading early Beaufighter exponent was Flt Lt John Cunningham of No 604 Sqn. A pre-war auxiliary, he claimed the type's first victory using the AI radar on 19 November 1940 when he brought down a Ju 88. Cunningham ended the war with 20 victories, 16 of them scored with the Beaufighter (*author's collection*)

Still displaying its delivery number on the nacelle after being flown to Middle Wallop in October 1940, Beaufighter IF R2101/NG-R later became the mount of Flt Lt John Cunningham in early 1941. He would claim ten victories while flying it (*P H T Green collection*)

night when Flt Lt John Cunningham and Sgt J R Phillipson of No 604 Sqn, flying R2098, claimed the Beaufighter's first victory using AI radar. It was also Cunningham's first victory and was vividly described by the man who was soon to be his navigator, 'Jimmy' Rawnsley;

'On the night of 20 November John and Phillipson went off on patrol. There were hostile aircraft about, and John was vectored after one of them. After a while he saw a concentration of searchlights on the clouds and he headed towards it. Phillipson was gazing intently at the cathode ray tubes, and then he got a good, firm contact. During the chase that followed, he was able to bring John into close range of the target they were following. John was searching the dark sky ahead, and for perhaps the tenth time he forced himself to look away from a cluster of stars that seemed to move in a different way from the others. As he did so, a vague, dark shape formed around them, only to dissolve again as he looked directly at it. He climbed a little closer and a silhouette took definite shape. At last, after all the long months of trial and error, of strain, worry and frustration, he had come to grips with the enemy. A few minutes later the stricken enemy bomber – it was a Junkers 88 – was plunging to earth, and for the first time an AI-equipped Beaufighter proved its worth on routine operational flying with a squadron.'

Their victim was Ju 88A B3+VL of 3./KG54. HQ Fighter Command was ecstatic, but to preserve the secrets of AI radar, the story of John Cunningham's incredible night vision was fed to the press, earning him his detested 'Cat's Eyes' nickname. Yet the number of nightfighter victories was to be relatively insignificant for the next three months, although training and greater experience eventually paid a handsome dividend, as is described in the following chapters.

The cockpit of a Beaufighter IF, with the aircraft's distinctive control column dominating the photograph (*author's collection*)

COUNTERING THE *BLITZ*

After their initial success, John Cunningham and J R Phillipson found action again on the evening of 23 December 1940. About 50 miles south of the Dorset coast they located a He 111 that was thought to be a pathfinder of KG 100. After a slow approach, Cunningham opened fire and the bomber plunged into cloud in a spectacular pyrotechnic display to mark his second success. The mid-winter nights found the nocturnal attacks on British cities increasing, and the means to counter this threat were pursued with urgency by Fighter Command.

By the start of 1941 Beaufighters had largely replaced Blenheims in the initial cadre of units, which were allocated to various sectors around the country. Split between Catterick, in Yorkshire, and Drem, near Edinburgh, was No 600 Sqn, led by pre-war Schneider Trophy winner Wg Cdr George Stainforth. At Digby was No 29 Sqn, which late in 1940 was joined by a talented young bomber pilot on a 'rest' tour. Flt Lt Guy Gibson is remembered by one of his groundcrew, LAC Fred Pedgeon;

'He came off a tour with Bomber Command's No 83 Sqn, and during his time with No 29 Sqn got three enemy aircraft. I well remember him for his sense of fair play, and total dedication to flying. Incidents like taking off full-bore at night from dispersal and just clearing the boundary trees in his efforts to get a Hun were also very memorable.'

Gibson's logbook recorded his first brush with the enemy in a Beaufighter on 11 December 1940;

'Chased bomber out over the sea and eventually shot at it with two short bursts at 800 yards 60 miles east of Mablethorpe. Identified as a Ju 88. No damage observed and enemy aircraft lost in cloud.'

Further south at Debden, in Essex, was No 25 Sqn, soon to be commanded by Wg Cdr David Atcherley. 'A' Flight commander was Sqn Ldr Harold 'Flash' Pleasance, a future ace who flew his first sortie in R2156 on the 9 December. On the south coast at Tangmere, in Sussex, was No 219 Sqn, which in February 1941 came under the control of Wg Cdr Tom Pike, who claimed six kills between March and June. Finally, at Middle Wallop, in Hampshire, was Sqn Ldr M F Anderson's No 604 Sqn, which was to find much early success, thus setting the pace for these first units.

It became evident from the start that constant practice was required to master the radar techniques and develop the cooperation so vital for successful nightfighting. John Cunningham later stated, 'It was a long hard grind and very frustrating. It was a struggle to continue flying on instruments at night. The essential was teamwork'. Close co-ordination and trust between pilot and radar operator (later re-styled as navigator-radio) was essential. Crews were left together to forge this bond, and many of the more successful remained so throughout the war.

The leading fighter pilot of the night *Blitz* was Sqn Ldr John Cunningham of No 604 Sqn, who claimed ten victories while flying Beaufighter IF R2101/NG-R from Middle Wallop between February and May 1941. Note the aircraft's wing aerials (*via R C B Ashworth*)

Perhaps the most famous of these early teams was that of Cunningham and his pre-war Auxiliary air gunner, Sgt 'Jimmy' Rawnsley. They flew their first operational Beaufighter patrol in mid December, and on 12 January 1941 made their first patrol in R2101/NG-R in which they were to find such success over the next few months. That night, under control of Tangmere GCI site (call-sign 'Boffin') they closed and identified a He 111, which they hit and damaged. But a cannon problem denied the pair their first victory together. Nonetheless, further dusk patrols were mounted over the Channel by the squadron in an effort to catch the pathfinders. Their first success was not long in coming, for on the evening of 15 February they downed a He 111, as depicted on the cover of this book. Two nights later No 219 Sqn was back scoring, as their diary noted;

'Do 17 destroyed by Sqn Ldr Little in R2154 with Sgt Pyne, which crashed between Maidenhead and Guildford, three of the crew becoming prisoners. The success came after a long period of hard luck and had a noticeable tonic effect on the whole squadron.'

It was the beginning of a busy period for the unit, which by May had claimed 20 destroyed, including four on 13 March, as better weather led to a marked increase in enemy activity. The diary of 'A' Flight of No 219 Sqn told of the changed fortunes that night;

'A red letter day for the Flight. Plt Off Hodgkinson brought down one, which crashed on landing, followed by Sgt Clandillon who brought one down shortly after, which also crashed. Sqn Ldr Little then took off and was in the air for 3 hr 10 min, during which time he had three engagements. The first enemy aircraft he gave a good burst, and it crashed into the sea near the Needles, this being later confirmed. Flt Lt Topham then took off and was vectored on to an enemy aircraft. He closed into 200 yards and gave them a burst. This enemy aircraft went down with one engine blazing. This too was later confirmed. During all this excitement the airfield was bombed twice!'

Johnny Topham's victim was He 111 6H+FK of 2./KGr 100, and its destruction set him well on course to become an ace. That night Flg Off Bob Braham, who became the RAF's most decorated fighter pilot, also claimed. He recalled his first Beaufighter victory in his autobiography;

'My second confirmed success occurred on the night of 13 March, a beautiful, cold, moonlit night. Sgt Ross, my Canadian AI operator, and I were scrambled towards the coast near Skegness. We levelled out at 15,000 ft. To gain surprise, we had to plan our approach to make it difficult for him to spot us. Ross had taken over the commentary, and was calmly directing me from the information on his scopes. I positioned myself to close the range, and my eyes strained to pick up an aircraft. As I stared I saw something moving. I blinked. Yes, there he was, a black object moving ahead of me and above. I could now vaguely make out twin rudders. I called GCI, "Tally Ho! I think it's a Dornier."

'Now I could make out the enemy, and identified him as a Dornier. I closed the range still further. I half expected to see tracer coming my way any minute because it was such a bright night. I eased back gently on the control column, allowing a little deflection, and pressed the firing button. The four cannons roared for a second then stopped. I saw a flash on the fuselage of the Dornier, where at least one of my shells had hit, and the enemy turned gently round to starboard back in the direction from which it had come. I pressed the firing button again, but nothing happened. Ross was already out of his seat, removing the 60-round magazines from the guns and working the firing mechanism to clear the trouble. I placed the gunsight on the target. I pressed the button, nothing happened – the oil in the guns was frozen. Again I eased back on the stick and closed the range to about 50 yards. He was taking no evasive action.

'Perhaps as I hadn't fired since the first short burst he thought he had lost me. I pressed the button, hoping that the guns would fire. The Beaufighter bucked as they roared away, and in a blinding sheet of flame the Do 17 blew up in my face. I was jubilant. As we turned for home we saw the flaming wreckage crash into the sea. Back at the airfield the news had gone ahead of us, and we stepped out of the aircraft to be surrounded by air and groundcrews.'

Braham was well regarded by his groundcrew, as one of them remembered;

'He was a man who would happily muck in and help in all sorts of ways. At Wellingore, near Digby, he would help refuel his aircraft when it was dispersed from the main parking area, before taxying back to the main site.'

On the south coast another distinguished nightfighter pilot, Roderick Chisholm of No 604 Sqn, claimed his first victory. He was described by a colleague as;

'Eternally restless in his search for perfection and never satisfied with himself or his operator. He forged an uneasy partnership with a happy-go-lucky sergeant by the name of W G Ripley.'

Chisholm too later wrote of his first victories;

'On the night of 13 March 1941, the unexpected happened. I destroyed two enemy aircraft. This was luck unbounded, and these were experiences which I know could never be equalled. For the rest of that night it was impossible to sleep. There was nothing I could talk about for days after. There was nothing else I could think about for weeks after.

'Ripley, my observer, got a close radar contact over to the left. I turned a little and could hardly believe my eyes, for there was another aircraft about 100 yards away, and on the same level. It was black, and its fish-like fuselage glistened dully in the moonlight. It was unmistakably a Heinkel. Converging rapidly, I turned to come behind and dropped below with an automatism that surprised me. My machine seemed to be on rails, so easily did it slide into position. I was able to creep up unmolested until I was within 100 yards and 45 degrees below. It looked enormous. The wings seemed to blot out the sky above me. Now a squat silhouette, it had lost its recognisable form. I saw four rows of exhausts, each with six stubs, and now and again one of them belched out a bigger flame than usual.

'The moment had come to shoot. It was now or never. Holding my breath, I eased the stick back a little and the Heinkel came down the

Flt Lt Bob Braham flew with No 29 Sqn during 1940-41 and made his first Beaufighter claim in March. He became an ace the following September, and went on to pioneer the use of nightfighters for bomber support duties with No 141 Sqn. With 29 enemy aircraft destroyed, he ended the war as the RAF's leading nightfighter pilot (*Norman Franks*)

windscreen and into the sight. It went too far and I found myself aiming above. Stick forward a bit and the sight came on it again. How ham-fisted this was! I pressed the firing button. There was a terrific shaking and banging, and to my surprise I saw flashes appearing, as it seemed, miraculously on the shape in front of me. I kept on firing and it turned away to the right, apparently helplessly and obviously badly damaged.

'My ammunition finished, I drew away farther to the right. I had overshot, and I could see the Heinkel over my left shoulder, still flying all right. Nothing happened – perhaps nothing was going to happen – and suddenly I thought that it was going to get away. And then I saw a lick of flame coming from the starboard engine. It grew rapidly and enveloped the whole engine and soon most of the wing. The machine turned east and started to go down slowly. It now looked like a ball of flame. We followed it down from 11,000 ft until, minutes later, it hit the sea, where it continued to burn.'

After refuelling, they were scrambled once more, and south of the Isle of Wight shot down another Heinkel. The following night No 29 Sqn gained further success when Gibson, in R2094, shot down a He 111 off Skegness in spite of constantly jamming cannon. Debris from his victim dented the Beaufighter's wings. Generally, however, March proved to be a frustrating month for No 604 Sqn. The unit gained a steady number of radar contacts, but victories proved elusive, although the skill of the crews, and particularly the radar operator/navigators, improved.

On the night of 3 April, Cunningham, who had recently been awarded a DFC, and Rawnsley were the last of No 604 Sqn's wave to get airborne. On checking in with 'Starlight', they immediately received a vector towards a homeward-bound bandit at 10,000 ft. It soon appeared on Rawnsley's tiny scope at a range of just over a mile. He took over to bring the Beaufighter in behind the bomber, just 2000 ft away. At that point Cunningham acquired it visually, and in spite of a violent thunderstorm, he closed in, as Rawnsley later described;

'John brought the gunsight onto the target. Then he opened fire, and almost at once the whole sky ahead of us seemed to dissolve in flame. Every slot and chink in the hull was lit by the lurid glow of the sea from the exploding Heinkel as we ploughed on through it. I looked over our starboard quarter and there I saw a terrible sight. The shattered Heinkel, with only one wing left, was spinning down vertically, spewing out as it went a helix of burning petrol.'

No 604 Sqn's star was now very much in the ascendant. The following night Flg Off Edward Crew, flying R2252, claimed his first Beaufighter victory in the form of a He 111 near Weston-super-Mare, in north Somerset. The future 13-victory ace was described by one of his contemporaries as 'a small, compact man who gave one the impression of being much larger than he was. He held himself erect, with a firm dignity, and when he spoke it was in a clipped, decisive manner'.

On 7 April John Cunningham became the first pilot to achieve five victories with the Beaufighter. The next night, with Rawnsley, he was patrolling at 15,000 ft, and as GCI was overloaded, they received permission to 'freelance'. Heading west towards some searchlights, they gained an AI contact to the left and below at about 8000 ft. As it crossed, Rawnsley instructed his pilot to make a starboard turn and dive. The curving profile brought them behind the unsuspecting He 111. It was hit and damaged, but then successfully evaded its attacker. The crew began searching for another, and soon gained a contact on a homeward-bound Heinkel, which they caught up with over Bournemouth. Rawnsley brought his pilot in. Going visual, Cunningham closed to about 80 yards before sending in a devastating burst of 20 mm cannon fire. It struck the belly of the bomber, which fell away and crashed.

No 25 Sqn also broke its duck on the 9th when Sgt Bennett took off from Wittering and shot down a Ju 88. No 604 Sqn's 'patch' also remained busy, and they continued to claim regularly. Cunningham brought down another He 111 on the 11th. As he watched it hit the ground, his only comment was, 'Good, that'll teach 'em to crack nuts in church'. Rory Chisholm was also on patrol, and he too shot down a Heinkel (from III./KG 55) south of Bournemouth to 'make ace'. He had claimed five kills in just 25 days.

A few days later, on 16 April, Cunningham confirmed his and Rawnsley's pre-eminent status when the pair brought down three He 111s. It had been an outstanding night, and soon afterwards he was awarded a DSO and Rawnsley a DFM. Further north No 29 Sqn was also busy, but it then moved to West Malling, in Kent, right in the path of incoming raids on London. Enjoying immediate success, Guy Gibson brought down a Heinkel, as he recorded in his logbook. 'One destroyed by lucky burst. It blew up. Another did the same before I could open fire'.

—— NEW SQUADRONS ——

As more Beaufighters became available, so older less capable types such as the Boulton Paul Defiant were replaced as new units formed with the Bristol nightfighter. In April No 141 Sqn at Ayr, in Scotland, began re-equipping, while at Wittering No 25 Sqn, led by Wg Cdr 'Batchy' Atcherley, began to get into its stride.

On the evening of 4 May Atcherley was under Langtoft GCI control and was vectored towards a target. He obtained AI contact at a range of 1.5 miles, becoming visual. Closing in to 100 yards, he identified a Ju 88. He fired two two-second bursts from both cannon and machine guns from dead astern. Almost immediately this caused a bright flash and a fire to break out in the fuselage, shedding pieces as it went down. Atcherley delivered the *coup de grace* with a long burst that sent Ju 88 Wk-Nr 3358 of 8./KG 1 to crash into the town of Bourne. It his was his first victory, but it demolished the Butcher's Arms pub, killing seven. Another crew downed an intruder near King's Lynn.

Three nights later, 'Flash' Pleasance and Sgt Bent in T4634 gained an AI contact north of the Wash. After a brief chase they saw a Dornier about 400 yards away. It then began a diving turn to port and Pleasance opened fire. The bomber levelled out and he attacked again, stopping the port engine and starting a fire. The intruder – Fw Wilhelm Lettenmeier's 2./NJG 2 Do 17Z-10 R4+GK – spiralled down to explode when it hit the ground near Boston. Two of the crew managed to bale out. This was the first of Pleasance's five victories with No 25 Sqn.

Off the south coast on 3 May, the CO of Tangmere's No 219 Sqn, Wg Cdr Tom Pike, opened what was to be a good month for them with his fourth victory, and a week later he described his fifth;

'I took off from Tangmere in Beaufighter R2253 at 0045 hrs, with Sgt Austin as AI operator, and was ordered to patrol Selsey Bill at 15,000 ft. Shortly after reaching my patrol line, Sgt Austin reported contact on his AI set. We followed, climbing to 18,000 ft whilst the enemy flew on a course towards London. The enemy was jinking most of the time and was finally overhauled and identified as a He 111. I attacked from about 250 yards dead astern and gave a short burst. The enemy immediately caught fire and a piece flew off and hit my Beaufighter. After a short time the enemy was seen to hit the ground and burst into flames.'

The night before Arthur Hodgkinson, now a pilot officer holding the DFC, finally became an ace. He reported;

'I was sent on a westerly vector at 16,000 ft but the enemy aircraft turned south and I was sent on various vectors. Climbing, we made AI contact, finding the enemy aircraft to starboard and below, with ourselves overtaking. I throttled back and lost height. I gave "Tally Ho!" and saw the enemy aircraft when about 600 yards away.

'When about 200 yards away we were shaken rather violently in the slipstream and the enemy aircraft opened fire, our windscreen being hit and splintered, rather obscuring the view. I dived slightly and came up under the enemy aircraft and gave a two- to three-second burst from 100 yards range. The enemy aircraft burst into flames in various places and we continued climbing and passed over the top of it. It was burning well in the cockpit, and the outline of the nose could be made out quite clearly, identifying it as a Heinkel 111. It then dived down into the sea, exploding just before hitting the sea.'

As he noted, at the close ranges required for an engagement, return fire could be both disconcerting and accurate.

It was at this time that the first Royal Canadian Air Force (RCAF) nightfighter unit, No 406 Sqn, was formed at Acklington under Wg Cdr D G 'Zulu' Morris. He was soon to make a name for himself, and his score gradually built up on Mk IIFs, many of which carried names based on the syllable 'Beau', among them *Beau Peep* and *Greta Gar-Beau*! Morris, like Tom Pike of No 219 Sqn, later became Fighter Command C-in-C.

A unit which eventually contained a large proportion of Czech exiles working up on Beaufighters was No 68 Sqn, stationed at High Ercall for

One of 1941's new Beaufighter units was No 68 Sqn, which was formed at High Ercall, where Mk IF X7583/WM-E is pictured. The aircraft arrived on 25 September, and was flown by several leading pilots, including Plt Offs M J Mansfeld and P F Allen. On the night of 28 April 1942 it was used by ace Wt Off Ladislaw Bobek to shoot down a Do 217 for his first victory (*RAFM*)

the defence of the Midlands. It was led by a seven-kill day fighter ace Wg Cdr the Hon Max Aitken, who was held in high regard. One of his newly-arrived young officers, Plt Off Eric Raybould, described what he found;

'The pilots were all ex-airline or Czech Air Force, and therefore older and much more experienced than their British counterparts. They were not interested in leave. They just wanted to fly and kill Germans – a thing they did very effectively.'

With new squadrons working-up, the experienced, but somewhat underemployed No 600 Sqn had moved south to Colerne in late April. There it began to receive the first Merlin-engined Beaufighter IIFs to enter service. It was some weeks before it was fully equipped, so when it first found action on the night of 16 May it was with a Mk IF. The pilot was future ace Flt Lt Archie Boyd. He had made his first Beaufighter flight in R2079 on 18 September 1940, and now described his first victory in his combat report;

'I was on patrol under control of Exeter when handed over to GCI Exminster and was put on the trace of a bandit when out to sea. After a series of vectors and an order to climb to 20,000 ft, I was told that the bandit was five miles ahead and flying north. I was then ordered to descend to 16,000 ft and to "flash". A blip was obtained, and after throttling right back, followed by a series of corrections from my operator, Flg Off Glegg, minimum range was rapidly reached and visual was obtained at 400 yards, and slightly above. The aircraft was identified as hostile, and I closed to 150-200 yards and opened fire from dead astern. A burst was given, and hits were observed in the fuselage and fires started. The aircraft was seen to

The RAF's leading Beaufighter unit was No 600 Sqn, although it made a slow start, not claiming its first victory until 16 May 1941. Twelve days later a Do 17 was shot down near Exeter by T4628/BQ-Z, which is the aircraft furthest from the camera in this formation (*IWM*)

Newly promoted Flt Lt Archie Boyd (right), who scored No 600 Sqn's first victory, is seen here with his navigator, Flg Off Alex Glegg, soon after both men had received the DFC in January 1942 (*P H T Green Collection*)

jettison its bombs, diving to port. I followed again and fired a further burst. The enemy aircraft dived in a flaming mass and exploded on impact near Honiton.'

Boyd's victim was Ju 88 V4+1R of 7./KG 1. Less fortunate was Sqn Ldr Pritchard, who was shot down by return fire, although the crew baled out, once again showing that these night encounters were by no means a sinecure for the fighter crews.

The increased effectiveness of the night defences was well shown on the night of 31 May/1 June. During the last major Luftwaffe raid of the night *blitz* on London, 24 aircraft were lost to nightfighters. One fell to Cunningham, who in T4625 left Middle Wallop and soon broke out into a clear starlit night after climbing through mist. Vectored onto an outbound bomber just west of base, in a very quick interception he gained a visual as it crossed from the left and opened fire. Using only 43 cannon rounds, he set it on fire and watched the flames spread as I./KG 27's He 111 1G+CH entered a shallow dive and hit the ground near Blandford. It was Cunningham's 13th victory. The crew then managed to land safely at Colerne just as the fog rolled in.

Raids still continued on other cities in the north and Midlands, giving trade to east coast squadrons. When the He 111s of KG 4, based at Leeuwarden, in Holland, raided Birmingham on 5 June, No 25 Sqn brought one down near Skegness. A few days later Sqn Ldr Pleasance claimed his third victory, shooting down a Ju 88C nightfighter. Another was brought down by the squadron that night too using a Mk IIF, which was one of only a handful to be issued to No 25 Sqn.

The squadron's most successful pilot from its Blenheim period, Kiwi Flt Lt Mike Herrick, gained his only Beaufighter victory on the 22nd. With Plt Off Yeomans, he left Wittering at 2230 hrs in R2777. They were heading back to base when Yeomans picked up a contact on his radar set. Four minutes later he brought Herrick into visual range, and the pilot identified a He 111 as he approached it from below at about 180 knots. To make sure, Herrick calmly formated off to one side before positioning astern once more just as the bomber made a diving turn to starboard.

With his gunsight unserviceable, Herrick sprayed the aircraft. It was another Ju 88C nightfighter (R4+JH) of 1./NJG 2, which was hit and set on fire. Two of the crew baled out, although one died. So too did the pilot, Fw Wiese, when it crashed at Deeping St James. It was the young New Zealander's fourth victory.

A few nights earlier, on 16/17 June, No 68 Sqn began scoring when Flt Lt Derek Pain succeeded in shooting down a KGr 100 He 111 near

Beaufighter IF T4637/NG-O of No 604 Sqn was used by Flt Lt Rory Chisholm to down a He 111 near Exeter on the night of 8 July 1941. This was his seventh, and final, Beaufighter kill. Chisholm was to make further claims while flying the Mosquito, however (*via author*)

Bath. It was also the first of his five Beaufighter victories.

The start of the campaign against Russia, however, meant that most of the *kampfgruppen* originally deployed against England had been moved. This, combined with the shorter nights, saw the large-scale night offensive against Britain brought to an end, although smaller raids continued to be flown by the remaining four *gruppen*.

— REDUCED ACTIVITY – CONTINUED ACTION —

Although reduced enemy activity saw a marked decline in the number of claims, Rory Chisholm wrote the following account on 9 July;

'My luck turned and we intercepted in quick succession two Heinkels heading for the Midlands. In the ensuing combats one was only damaged, but the second blew up after a short burst, like a match being struck, and spun down, leaving only a plume of smoke.'

It was his final Beaufighter victory, although No 604 Sqn was certainly keeping its score mounting steadily as on 7 July Flt Lt Edward Crew (in R2143), with Sgt Norman Guthrie, had shot down a Ju 88 and a He 111 during a raid on Southampton, elevating him to ace status.

Later in the month No 255 Sqn began conversion to Beaufighter IIs. The first two arrived on the 22nd, and by 6 August there were 18 on strength. While it was working up, however, a detachment from No 604 Sqn moved across to Coltishall to act as cover. John Cunningham had recently been promoted to wing commander to lead the unit, and he was replaced as 'B' Flight CO by Sqn Ldr 'Rory' Chisholm. Rawnsley was commissioned to become navigator leader.

No 604 Sqn's first success on the east coast fell to its new CO when Rawnsley gained a fleeting AI contact. Turning hard and diving, Cunningham brought the Beaufighter head-on to a He 111. His first burst started a fire in its bomb-bay, forcing the crew to bale out as it nosed over into the Wash. Just before landing back at base, they were sent out after another contact – yet another Heinkel. They damaged it, but were hit by return fire and had to break off.

That same day, 22 July, No 255 Sqn lost its CO, Sqn Ldr R Smith, in a crash and the following day was declared non-operational to enable it to complete conversion. No 604 Sqn's detachment was ordered to remain for a further period. Despite its troubled transition from the Defiant and Hurricane onto the Beaufighter, No 255 Sqn was receiving some talented pilots. These included pre-war Kiwi instructor pilot Flt Lt John Player from No 54 Operational Training Unit and Czech Battle of France/Britain ace

To aid production, the Beaufighter IIF was fitted with Merlin engines, although these powerplants significantly degraded the aircraft's handling characteristics. No 255 Sqn began replacing its Defiants with Beaufighter IIFs in late July 1941, and R2402/YD-G was issued to the unit on 5 August. The squadron had a difficult conversion period, losing two COs in accidents (*RAF Official*)

This rare in-flight view of a Beaufighter IIF shows an unidentified No 409 Sqn aircraft undertaking a training sortie during daylight hours. The photograph was taken in late 1941 when the unit was based in Lincolnshire (*D M Dixon*)

The only Polish nightfighter unit was No 307 Sqn, which began receiving Beaufighters IIFs in the summer of 1941. It was based at Exeter for the defence of Plymouth and the West Country, and although it achieved numerous successes, none of its pilots became aces (*via M W Payne*)

The RAAF's only nightfighter unit was No 456 Sqn, which began swapping its Defiant Is for Beaufighter IIFs in September 1941. The unit's first CO was Battle of Britain Spitfire ace Wg Cdr Gordon Olive, who made his first operational Beaufighter patrol in this aircraft, T3017/RX-B, on 17 December. He subsequently flew the aircraft on numerous other occasions too (*via J W Bennett*)

Flt Sgt Eduard Prchal. Another RCAF unit, No 409 Sqn at Coleby Grange, also received its first Beaufighter II at the end of August.

The Merlin-engined Beaufighter II lived up to its reputation for evil handling when No 409 Sqn's first CO, Sqn Ldr N B Petersen, was lost in an accident and replaced by Wg Cdr Paul Davoud. August also saw the Polish-manned No 307 'Lwowski' Sqn at Exeter begin receiving Beaufighter IIs. This unit also had problems with the aircraft. Soon afterwards, another Defiant squadron also began re-equipping with Mk IIs when, on 26 September, the Australian-manned No 456 Sqn at Valley received its first aircraft. Led by Spitfire ace Wg Cdr Gordon Olive (an Australian who had initially served in the RAAF, before joining the RAF in 1937), it began operations at the end of November. Several future aces also flew with the unit, namely Flt Lt George Coleman and Plt Off Mike Gloster. Both were later to make their mark.

No 406 Sqn achieved its first victory on 1 September when Flg Off R C 'Moose' Fumerton (in R2336), with Sgt Pat Bing, gained the first of his 14 night victories. The RCAF Official History records;

The first RCAF nightfighter unit to form was No 406 Sqn, which was equipped with Beaufighter IIFs. The unit claimed its first success on the night of 1 September 1941 (*Canadian Forces*)

'They intercepted a Ju 88 which was attempting to attack Tyneside and, stalking the raider from cloud to cloud, finally dived and opened fire before the Hun had any idea that a nightfighter was in the vicinity. The first burst, fired from behind and below the Junkers at a range of only 50 yards, set the starboard engine afire and raked the fuselage from stem to stern. After a second attack the enemy aircraft exploded in mid-air and fell in

flaming pieces. The fuselage cross from this aircraft was cut out and became No 406's scoreboard.'

Fumerton would later become the RCAF's leading nightfighter ace.

That same night No 604 Sqn had its final action during the Coltishall detachment when Wg Cdr Cunningham delivered a devastating attack on a Ju 88 to bring it down into the sea 30 miles off the coast.

On 4 September No 406 Sqn's CO Wg Cdr Morris, with Sgts Rix and Hardy, got airborne in a Beaufighter V at 2200 hrs and landed just before midnight. This was one of the very few operational sorties flown by a turret-armed Beaufighter V. Only R2274 and R2306 were built with a pair of cannon and the four wing-mounted machine guns supplanted by a turret with four 0.303-in guns behind the pilot. The latter drastically reduced performance and the Mk V was abandoned. Morris wrote;

'Chased many aircraft but unable to gain AI contact. The enemy was apparently circling over a large area out to sea off the Tyne, and GCI was unable to bring the fighter into proper contact.'

Activity in No 406 Sqn's 'patch' continued, and a few days later Fumerton and Bing again intercepted a raider, this time a He 111. It was damaged by two bursts of cannon fire before it escaped into cloud. Of the nightfighting role, Bing said;

'Nightfighting is a specialised form of aerial warfare unlike any other. It calls for high efficiency on the part of the pilot and observer and a great deal of co-operation within the crew, and between the crew and the operations controller on the ground.'

On 10 September future ace Plt Off Michael Kinmonth had his first contact with the Luftwaffe when he chased an AI contact, but could not gain a visual. He subsequently enjoyed better success with No 89 Sqn in the Mediterranean during 1942, scoring seven Beaufighter victories.

After its troubled start, No 255 Sqn began operations at the end of September. The last day of the month also saw 'Zulu' Morris of No 406 Sqn open his account. The RCAF official history records;

'The RAF officer from South Africa set an example to his pilots by destroying three raiders in two nights when the Luftwaffe attempted further raids on Tyneside at the end of September and beginning of October. During the night of 30 September 1941, Morris accounted for

No 406 Sqn's first CO was RAF officer Wg Cdr Douglas 'Zulu' Morris, who made at least four successful claims during his tour. He was well-regarded throughout the Air Force, and after the war became C-in-C, Fighter Command (*Canadian Forces*)

On 4 September 1941 'Zulu' Morris made one of the very few operational sorties in the turret-armed Beaufighter V. No 406 Sqn had this one (R2274) on strength for a short time for trials, which proved unsuccessful (*Bristol Aircraft*)

a Ju 88, and two nights later a He 111 and a Do 217. He was awarded the DFC and his observer, Sgt Rix, the DFM.'

They were to make another claim together in 1942.

Archie Boyd of No 600 Sqn, now a squadron leader and flight commander, was in action again soon afterwards, shooting down a He 111 off the Cornish coast.

On 12 October a significant personality made his first night claims. Exiled Czech Plt Off Miroslav Mansfeld, serving with No 68 Sqn, was flying off the Welsh coast near Holyhead with Sgt Slavomil Janacek in R2248/WM-S when they were vectored onto a Ju 88. Damaging the bomber, he then destroyed two more within five minutes to set Mansfeld on the way to becoming the leading Czech night ace with 8.5 kills.

Much to their delight, fellow exiles serving with No 307 Sqn at Exeter also began to find action with their new aircraft. On 28 October Sgt Turzanski, with Sgt Ostrowski, fired on a Heinkel without apparent effect. Their luck changed on 1 November when they intercepted and shot down two Dorniers. The second was a very early Do 217E-2, Wk-Nr 1123 U5+EM, of 4./KG 2, which came down in the sea off Sidmouth. The pair were successful again on the 28th, and claimed their fourth victim in early 1942. Frustratingly, the fifth success never came, although Boleslaw Turzanski was to remain the war's leading Polish nightfighter.

On the same night as Turzanski opened his account, No 409 Sqn did the same. Appropriately, the first kill fell to unit CO, Wg Cdr Paul Davoud. He wrote at the time;

'I closed to 200 yards, identified a Dornier 217, and fired a short burst, observing hits on the starboard mainplane. The Dornier returned fire and, having closed to about 200 yards, I fired two long bursts, seeing the second hit his starboard engine. Just before the Dornier entered cloud, a big explosion blew his right engine and wing off. I pulled up to avoid a collision and the Dornier fell burning straight into the sea.'

Also making his scoring debut that night was No 68 Sqn's Plt Off Mervyn Shipard, who would become the leading RAAF night ace. During a detachment to Valley while No 456 Sqn worked up, Shipard and his navigator, Sgt Douggie Oxby, intercepted a raid on Liverpool and shot down Lt Lens' He 111H F8+KR of 7./KG 40.

The most successful Polish nightfighter pilot was No 307 Sqn's Sgt Boleslaw Turzanski, who made his first claims on 1 November 1941 when he brought down two Dorniers – hence his gesture to the camera in this photograph. He later claimed two more victories, but his fifth kill never came (*W Matusiak*)

Beaufighter IIF T3145/KP-K of No 409 Sqn, pictured at a muddy Coleby Grange during late 1941. It was the regular mount of the squadron CO, Wg Cdr P Y Davoud, who claimed the unit's first victory on the night of 1 November 1941 (*P H T Green Collection*)

BAEDEKER AND BISCAY

Compared with the terrors of the previous year, the winter of 1941-42 was much quieter, with fewer night attacks and a much more sophisticated night defence system now in place. There were still raids on industrial complexes and ports, as well as 'tip and run' attacks on the south coast. And from the night of 24/25 April 1942, there were also attacks on lightly-defended cathedral cities – the infamous Baedeker raids. The Australians in No 456 Sqn had been extremely frustrated at Valley throughout this period, but in the New Year the unit finally broke its duck, as the squadron history recounted;

'The tide finally turned for the squadron on the night of 10 January 1942, with No 456's first taste of victory. "A" Flight CO, Sqn Ldr Hamilton, and Plt Off Dan Norris-Smith (T3014), were scrambled at 2210 hrs and vectored by Soapy GCI towards an enemy raid. After a seven-minute chase, the Beaufighter caught its prey. The target was identified as a fast and manoeuvrable Dornier Do 217 bomber, and was despatched in flames after two bursts. The raider, from *Kampfgeschwader* 40, crashed at Arbury, in Merseyside. The endless night training and practice intercepts had finally paid off.'

A month later, No 141 Sqn, defending the north-east from Acklington, had its first success since re-equipping. On the night of 15/16 February Flg Off 'Ben' Benson and Sgt Lewis Brandon (in X7577) caught a Do 217E-4 (Wk-Nr 1187/U5+BD) of KG 2, flown by the *Gruppenkommodore* Maj Gerhard Klostermann, off Northumberland. Brandon described the encounter after the war;

'As we levelled out, Ben automatically opened the throttles. We were closing in perfectly. The blip showed almost dead ahead now. My eyes took a moment to become accustomed to the dark, then I saw, just above and to starboard, the vague silhouette of an aircraft. It was a Dornier 217 all right. It seemed strange that it should be completely indifferent to the presence of a Beaufighter so close. As it passed though the gun-sight, Ben turned the Beau to follow the Dornier. All hell broke loose as he pressed the gun button. Ben had given it a two-second burst of gun-fire but, although the Dornier began to lose height, we had seen no strikes. We were now following it in a very sharp dive, and Ben gave it two more bursts from a range of about 300 ft. This time we saw

One of the successful Czech teams to fly the Beaufighter with No 68 Sqn was Flg Off Ladislaw Bobek DFC (right) and his navigator Wt Off Bohuslav Kovaric DFM (left). They achieved a score of five destroyed, one probable and three damaged between April 1942 and March 1943 (*Zdenek Hurt*)

strikes all along the fuselage and tail unit, from which there was a great red flash which illuminated the whole aircraft.'

They lost sight of it but, after landing, two ground reports confirmed their victim had crashed off Blyth. It was Benson's second kill, and he was to become an ace the following year flying Mosquitos.

As 1942 progressed, more new units were re-equipped with the Beaufighter. One was No 153 Sqn, based in Northern Ireland, and a third Canadian squadron, No 410, also began receiving Beaufighter IIs in April. Its pilots included future ace Flt Lt Tim Woodman. Another new unit was No 125 Sqn, which had many Newfoundlanders on strength. On 25/26 April its training was interrupted by the Baedeker raids on Bath. On the second night the squadron flew layer patrols over the city, claiming one probable and one damaged, before completing its conversion at Fairwood Common in mid-May.

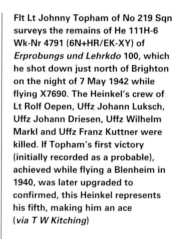

Shortly before midnight on 28 April a large force of German bombers passed over Wells-next-the-Sea, heading for Norwich. No 68 Sqn scrambled nine Beaufighters from Coltishall. Among them was X7583/WM-E, flown by Wt Off Ladislaw Bobek with Sgt Kovaric. They chased a Do 217 for 20 minutes before bringing it down off Great Yarmouth. It was the first of Bobek's five victories. Two nights later the Luftwaffe returned, and he shared in the destruction of a Do 217 with Plt Off Miro Mansfeld, who was also credited with two He 111s to make him an ace. Both were hit by return fire. Norwich was raided again on 8 May, and over the south coast that night Flt Lt Johnny Topham of No 219 Sqn gained what is thought to have been his fifth victory when he downed Ltn Oepen's He 111H-6 6N+HR of *Erprobungs und Lehrkdo* 100.

No 604 Sqn, still at Middle Wallop, continued to score occasionally during this period. Edward Crew, and his navigator Basil Duckett, gained two victories on successive nights in early May, as a contemporary account described;

'From the first of these Crew came back with his victim's trailing aerial wrapped around his starboard airscrew. The second battle developed into quite a protracted affair. He was given contact by an inland GCI rejoicing in the delightful name of "Moonglow", and the chase

The first unit to receive the Beaufighter VIF in the spring of 1942 was No 255 Sqn at Honiley. This aircraft is X7966/YD-P, and it was regularly flown between June and August by Plt Off Douglas Greaves, who became No 255 Sqn's first ace after it moved to North Africa (*No 255 Sqn Records*)

Between March and September 1942, one of No 255 Sqn's flight commanders was Sqn Ldr Dennis Hayley-Bell, who is seen (right) with his navigator, Flt Sgt Vezzell, in front of their aircraft at Honiley in July 1942. As well as making claims on conventional nightfighters, Hayley-Bell had also flown experimental mine-laying Harrows and Havocs during 1941 (*No 255 Sqn Records*)

Wg Cdr John Cunningham (right) and Flg Off Jimmy Rawnsley of No 604 Sqn stand by the tail of their Beaufighter. Barely discernable above the fin flash are 16 small swastikas, denoting Cunningham's score up to that time. He claimed four more while flying the Mosquito, and is perhaps the best-known RAF nightfighter pilot of World War 2 (*P H T Green collection*)

went on until they were well out to sea. The Dornier twisted and dived and fought hard to get away but Crew was not to be shaken off. He ran out of ammunition, but he still held on to the frantic bomber while Basil Duckett struggled to reload the other guns. They were down to 2000 ft when he saw the enemy aircraft hit the sea in a flurry of smoke and steam.'

These were the last of his eight Beaufighter victories. By then Crew's squadron was flying the improved Beaufighter VIF, which had first arrived with No 255 Sqn during March. No 604 Sqn was, however, now receiving the new AI Mk VII, which featured a plastic nose for the radar scanner.

John Cunningham's final Beaufighter kill came during daylight hours on 23 May, when he and Rawnsley were ordered to patrol off Swanage against 'tip and run' raiders on a dank day full of low cloud and drizzle. They were vectored onto a contact that materialised as a He 111, flown by KGr 100's CO, Hpt Laner, which evaded most of the Beaufighter's efforts to gain a firing position. Eventually Cunningham succeeded, however, taking his tally of Beaufighter kills to 16 (14 He 111s and two Ju 88s), with a further two as probables and six more damaged.

The following night saw No 68 Sqn in action again over East Anglia when Ladislaw Bobek (in V8283/WM-M) damaged a Ju 88 while his CO, Wg Cdr Max Aitken, shot down a Do 217 for his second night victory. Other pilots got two more to make it a good night for the squadron.

In early June No 410 Sqn flew its first Beaufighter operations, but it only had occasional scrambles in its quiet sector. Much to its relief, No 141 Sqn moved south from Acklington to Tangmere towards the end of the same month, and things proved much busier at the south coast base, particularly against Luftwaffe 'tip and run' raiders.

No 68 Sqn at Coltishall remained one of the more active units, shooting down three Dorniers on the 23 June, for example. Soon

afterwards No 488 Sqn RNZAF, which had suffered heavy losses flying Buffaloes and Hurricanes in the Far East in January 1942, began forming at Church Fenton. Led by eight-victory Kiwi ace Wg Cdr R M Trousdale DFC, with Sqn Ldrs Johnny Gardner and Paul Rabone (four victories, and who later became an ace during 1943) as flight commanders, the unit encountered many difficulties, including a shortage of trained ground staff, as it worked up over the next few months. Also at Church Fenton under Wg Cdr 'Flash' Pleasance was No 25 Sqn, which became active once more with the Baedeker offensive.

On the other side of the country, No 125 Sqn flew patrols over the Irish Sea, and early on 27 June, Defiant ace Sqn Ldr Desmond Hughes (in Beaufighter IIF V8141) led a sweep off the southern Irish coast during which the controller advised them of a hostile contact off the coast of County Waterford. Hughes made two attacks on Ju 88D Wk-Nr 430211 4T+MH of *WeKuSta* 51, which was flying a weather reconnaissance mission. He shot the aircraft down to claim No 125's first confirmed victory. It was also Hughes' first with the Beaufighter. Of the Merlin-engined Mk IIF he told the author;

'I quite enjoyed the Beaufighter II, although it had a horrific "swing" on take-off unless one opened one throttle a full two inches ahead of the other. All first solos were interesting to watch, one culminating in a dash between two hangars!'

No 68 Sqn enjoyed another good night during raids on Great Yarmouth and King's Lynn on 23 July when the unit sortied no fewer than ten Beaufighters. Bobek and Kovarik destroyed a Do 217, while Max Aitken also got one, plus a Ju 88. A few days later he was awarded a well-deserved DSO. The unit made more claims over the next month.

No 96 Sqn was also declared operational on 23 July when it flew three sorties. Four nights later Flg Off 'Jamie' Jameson, who had joined No 125 Sqn in June, had his first combat during the enemy *blitz* on the South Wales ports of Cardiff and Swansea. After a chase he destroyed a He 111, bringing down

Beaufighter IF X7842/WM-P was named *BIRMINGHAM CIVIL DEFENCE*, which it certainly took literally! On its first sortie with No 68 Sqn on 26 June 1942, Plt Off J W Gough (a future V1 ace) shot down a Do 217, and when flown by Plt Off Cleaver two nights later it accounted for another. Standing at the extreme left in this shot is regular pilot Plt Off Raybould, who downed a third Dornier on 29 July. He told the author, 'I was able to go out and inspect the wreckage. There wasn't much left, but we were able to bring back some trophies, and a tail fin served as the squadron scoreboard. My aircraft seemed to be lucky, for everybody who borrowed it seemed to shoot something down' (*E B Raybould*)

No 25 Sqn was based at Church Fenton for much of 1942-43, and Beaufighter IF X7876/ZK-F was one of its aircraft. It is seen here during maintenance before going onto night readiness. This photograph was taken after the roundels had been changed to Type 'C' in July 1942, but before the introduction of the grey-green camouflage in the autumn (*via J D R Rawlings*)

Wrexham-based No 96 Sqn was one of the last Defiant units to be re-equipped, in May 1942. Seen here dispersed at its base, Beaufighter IIF T3415/ZJ-M was the aircraft which flight commander Sqn Ldr Dickie Haine (three victories) always wanted to be allocated (*R C Haine*)

Flg Off Jamie Jameson began his combat career with No 125 Sqn, but after converting to Mosquitos with No 488 Sqn, his score rose to 11 destroyed to make him the war's leading RNZAF nightfighter pilot (*P H T Green Collection*)

a second off Milford Haven a week later. These were the first of his total of 11, making him New Zealand's leading nightfighter pilot.

In early September Wt Off Lofty Hamer of No 141 Sqn destroyed a He 111 off St Alban's Head, but return fire wounded him and set his starboard engine on fire. Because his navigator was a non-swimmer, he elected to fly the crippled aircraft until it was over the Isle of Wight, allowing Flt Sgt Walsh to bale out just before he lost control and crashed. On his last radio call he said, 'Afraid I'm finished – I'll have to go, over'. He had gallantly sacrificed his own chance of saving himself and was recommended for the Victoria Cross, although it was not approved.

Meanwhile, on the east coast No 25 Sqn was claiming steadily. On 24 August, flying a new Mk VIF, Flg Off Joe Singleton caught a Do 217

In 1943 veteran frontline pilot Sqn Ldr Dennis Hayley-Bell (three victories) served as a flight commander with several nightfighter units. During the late summer he was with No 125 Sqn at Exeter, and among the aircraft he flew on operational patrols was Beaufighter VIF MM849/VA-T, seen here at its dispersal (*via Larry Milberry*)

This splendid view of No 409 Sqn's Beaufighter VIF KP-Q was taken around September 1942, and shows all the various transmitting and receiving radar aerials to advantage (*D M Dixon*)

Beaufighter VIF X8016/JT-G of No 256 Sqn displays the new green/grey nightfighter camouflage introduced in late 1942. Part of the squadron's detachment at Ballyhalbert, Northern Ireland, it was flown in December 1942 by future Mosquito ace Flg Off J W 'Ian' Allan (*B J Wild*)

Baedeker raider east of Bourne. He inflicted severe damage on 2./KG 2's U5+SK, causing it to crash near King's Lynn with the loss of its crew. In Scotland No 410 Sqn opened its account too with an aircraft from KG 2, and by the end of September the German unit had lost almost three-quarters of its complement.

By now most nightfighter units had Beaufighter VIs, including No 125 Sqn, which in early October detached four aircraft to Sumburgh, in the Shetland Islands, to intercept enemy Atlantic weather reconnaissance flights. On the night of 27 October 'Jamie' Jameson damaged a Ju 88, while on 4 November one was destroyed in a daylight interception. Squadron records recall;

'After experiencing tracer fire, Sqn Ldr Hughes opened fire from dead astern and strikes were observed all over the enemy aircraft. Flg Off Turnbull then attacked and numerous strikes were seen. The Ju 88 went down into the sea in flames and disappeared.'

The Ju 88 was from *WeKuSta* 1, and Hughes' share in its destruction represented his seventh success. It was the first of 12.5 kills for Canadian John Turnbull. Six days later six-victory ace Flt Lt Jim Bailey claimed another. Again, the action was described in the squadron records:

'When 118 miles east of Montrose, the enemy aircraft was sighted ten miles to the east, flying north at 13,000 ft. The Beaufighter was as 14,000 ft, flying north-north-east. The enemy aircraft opened fire at 1000 yards without success. Flt Lt Bailey closed astern and opened fire from 450 yards, scoring hits on the port engine of the enemy aircraft, which was identified as a Ju 88. From a range of 250 yards Flt Lt Bailey was hit in the right ear by a bullet, and as his port engine was cutting he turned for base.'

The following day, Daily Intelligence referred to the Ju 88 'as having been destroyed by No 125 Sqn'.

By this time the Mosquito was beginning to replace the Beaufighter in some units. No 25 Sqn's first example arrived during October, and it was fully equipped by January 1943. One of the shortest-lived Beaufighter units was No 256 Sqn. Being in the north-west, it saw little action, and during January 1943, for example, flew only three patrols. One was on the 17th when Flt Lt Dennis Hughes, who later became an ace on Mosquitos, scrambled despite the somewhat ironic comment in the squadron records that 'the raid was on London!' Over the capital, however, No 29 Sqn had a memorable night when, against a force of 50 bombers, the unit mounted 27 sorties. Squadron CO Wg Cdr Michael Wight-Boycott was soon engaged. He later said of the engagement;

'The curious thing about the first one I shot down was that, although London was throwing up a terrific amount of flak and there were any number of searchlights about, I don't remember seeing any of them at all. I was looking up all the time to find the enemy silhouetted against the bright moonlit sky. We'd just popped up out of a thin layer of cloud and there was the Dornier, a sort of grey colour. I fired a long burst and saw an explosion behind the pilot's cockpit. It seemed to go straight down, and I tried to follow – so steeply that my observer came out of his seat. When the Dornier crashed, three brilliant white blobs appeared to jump out of the ground. That was Dornier number one.

'On the next patrol nothing happened at all, except my observer complained about the hardness of his seat! We got Dornier number two during our second alert. It must have been about four in the morning. He was travelling very fast and jinking violently. He didn't keep a straight course for more than a few seconds at a time. There was no cloud about now. It was a good night for interception, and I managed to get a fairly long burst. He caught fire and slowed up very quickly. I got so close to him that I was caught in his slipstream and rolled onto my back, but I managed to avoid colliding with him. By the time we were the right way up he'd hit the ground and was blazing away.

'Then came Dornier number three. Again, I got in a long burst amidships. There was a yellowish explosion and down he went. As he did so he fired about a second's burst – two streams of red tracer – but they went nowhere near us. Number four was a Junkers 88, and the most spectacular of the night. We found him somewhere in the Croydon area. My cannon shells set both his engines on fire, and flames spread along his

Another long-time Beaufighter squadron still flying the Mk IF in late 1942 was West Malling-based No 29, which operated V8324/RO-B. Prominent on the nose of this aircraft are the Disney cartoon characters *Bambi* and *Thumper*. The aircraft was sometimes flown by Plt Off 'Togs' Mellersh, who later gained seven victories on the type in the Mediterranean with No 600 Sqn in 1943, followed by at least 39 V1s flying Mosquito XIIIs with No 96 Sqn in 1944. Mellersh's final kill was a Ju 88 destroyed in April 1945 while flying a Mosquito XXX with the Fighter Interception Development Unit (*Air Ministry*)

wing and back to the fuselage. They lit up the sky so clearly that we could see his black crosses. And we saw four crew bale out, one after another. As the bomber went down you could see all the streets lit up, and when it hit there was a terrific flash. Home we went, pleased, but wondering what luck the rest of the squadron had had.'

Wight-Boycott was credited with three destroyed and one damaged. He was awarded an immediate DSO for his feat. The following year he became an ace flying Mosquitos.

BOMBER SUPPORT

Just before Christmas 1942 No 141 Sqn, at Ford, gained a dynamic new CO when Wg Cdr Bob Braham arrived. His first taste of action with his new unit came a little after 2300 hrs on 23 January when he and his navigator, Flg Off 'Sticks' Gregory, took off in V8258, fitted with an AI Mk VII radar. South of Eastbourne, they closed on an unsuspecting Dornier, as Braham's report describes;

'I recognised the enemy aircraft as a Do 217, and at 2359 hrs gave him a three-second deflection burst of cannon and machine guns from slightly above and 20 degrees astern from 1000 ft, closing to 900 ft. There were many strikes on the enemy aircraft's fuselage and return fire was silenced. As the opportunity presented itself, I gave three more deflection bursts of cannon and machine guns, each of about three seconds, and closing from 900 to 600 ft. The first of these bursts was from below, and resulted in many strikes on the fuselage. The next was from the same relative position, when more strikes on the fuselage were soon followed by smoke. The last burst from slightly above and astern was delivered at about 0015 hrs, and resulted in the enemy aircraft diving straight down with smoke pouring from it. I dived after it and I saw a large splash in the sea ahead of us about 8-10 miles south-west of Dungeness.'

This was Braham's 13th victory, and his first with No 141 Sqn.

The following month the squadron moved west to Predannack to conduct offensive long-range fighter patrols over enemy territory and over the South-West Approaches and Biscay. During mid-March 1943 it mounted its first offensive night 'Ranger' operation. Other nightfighter units participated, including No 96 Sqn. No 141 Sqn also began 'Instep' operations in support of Coastal Command patrol aircraft over Biscay.

Over England, the Beaufighter squadrons also maintained their defensive shield, typically during the February 1943 *blitz* on Swansea, when Flt Lt Jamie Jameson claimed his final Beaufighter victory on the

Behind these four pilots from Newfoundland at Fairwood Common in January 1943 sits Beaufighter VIF V8515/VA-S of No 125 Sqn. It was while flying this aircraft on the night of 11 February that Flg Off Jamie Jameson shot down a Do 217 near Swansea for his third, and final, Beaufighter success (*P H T Green collection*)

11th. Also up that night was his CO, Battle of Britain Hurricane pilot Wg Cdr Rupert Clerke, who, the unit diary said, was 'up on a GCI practice, and gained a contact obtained uncontrolled. The pilot believed the aircraft to be a Do 217, and gave a burst of 12 seconds from 400 yards dead astern. Many strikes were observed and the Dornier dived away burning from both engines. It crashed near Yeovil.'

This was Clerke's sixth claim, and his first of two on the Beaufighter.

One of the most significant Beaufighter units during 1943 was No 141 Sqn, which pioneered the offensive use of nightfighters in the bomber support role in the spring of that year. Seen earlier in 1943 is Mk VIF V8253/TW-T, which flew its first patrol with the squadron on 21 January. Its pilot on this occasion was Flg Off Le Boutte *(via Larry Milberry)*

One month later, on 14 March, fellow day fighter ace Sqn Ldr J S 'Black' Morton of No 219 Sqn, intercepted and shot down a Do 217 over the North Sea off Hartlepool. He confided to his diary how he had scored his first night victory;

'We closed gradually, however, and eventually had a visual on exhaust flames at about 3000 ft. The enemy aircraft was nicely above us, and weaving about like mad. Suddenly, a shower of red sparks came out of him and ripped underneath us. I immediately opened fire as, not only had he obviously seen us, but we were now very close indeed. We were dead astern, and there were a good few strikes on the starboard side and top of the fuselage and the starboard centre section out to the engine, including a very bright flash from the engine. I was about to take a nice 20-degree shot from his port quarter when there was a terrific scream from my starboard motor as the revs went right off the clock. The last I saw of him he was going down hard and trailing lights, but still flying okay.'

Morton then went on to describe how the port engine also stopped, and how he fought to keep the aircraft steady to allow his navigator to struggle out before parachuting to safety. But Charles Strange had landed in the cold sea and been unable to get into his dinghy. By the time he was found later in the day he had died from exposure. Morton closed his diary entry with the words, 'I claimed a very shaky "damaged" on the Hun, but apparently he was seen to go straight in in flames, so we got a "confirmed" after all'. Shortly afterwards the squadron began moving to North Africa.

No 141 Sqn continued on its offensive sojourn in the west until it was recalled for a new offensive role – intruder patrols over enemy territory using the Serrate radar detection equipment. This allowed a Beaufighter crew to home in on enemy nightfighter radar emissions. The unit duly moved to Wittering at the end of April 1943 in preparation for flying bomber support operations. On 14 June No 141 Sqn began Serrate operations when five aircraft patrolled the Luftwaffe nightfighter bases at Deelen, Eindhoven and Gilze-Rijn, in Holland, to cover a bombing raid on Oberhausen. Flg Off Gregory, leading from the front as usual, shot down a Bf 110 over the Zuider Zee, and a Ju 88 was damaged near Schouwen the following night to begin a successful period for the squadron in its new role.

Further kills followed, and on the night of 22/23 June Flg Off Howard Kelsey destroyed a Bf 110 near Rijssen for the first of his nine victories.

Displaying its thimble nose radome, No 604 Sqn's Beaufighter VIF MM856/NG-C was being flown by the unit CO, Wg Cdr Michael Constable-Maxwell, on a day sortie on 23 August 1943 when he downed a Ju 88 over the central North Sea to achieve his first Beaufighter victory (*J Wilkinson*)

Seen here sitting on the wing of a Mosquito, Wg Cdr Michael Constable-Maxwell achieved five kills to add to his previous day fighter claims while serving as No 604 Sqn's CO. On the ground is his long-time navigator, Flt Lt John Quinton, who after the war when serving as an instructor was posthumously awarded the George Cross (*via G R Pitchfork*)

Two nights later his CO, in X8147, also shot down a Bf 110 near Gilze-Rijn, while on 26/27 June Kelsey got another near Hardenburgh. On 3/4 July No 141 Sqn's most successful crew, Flg Offs Harold White and Michael Allen, opened their account when they damaged a Bf 110 over Aachen. Nine days later White claimed his first kill when he downed a *Zerstörer* near Rheims. He recorded at the time;

'We made landfall over the French coast at Ault. When we were about eight miles south east of Rheims at 0200 hrs we saw a Me 110 3000 ft ahead of us, flying straight and level at 10,000 ft. We at once dived down to get dead astern and slightly below. Opening fire at 750 ft, we slowly closed to 600 ft and I fired a second burst from our cannon and machine gun. There were strikes on both engines and on the fuselage, and a moment later the whole aircraft exploded in flames, splitting into two burning pieces, one of which was blown right behind us. We watched both pieces strike the ground, where they continued to burn.'

His victim was the 31-victory *experte* and Knights Cross holder Maj Herbert Rauh of II./NJG 4. A month later, on 17/18 August, No 141 Sqn's patrols supported the raid on the rocket research establishment at Peenemunde, on the German Baltic coast. Ten Serrate-equipped Beaufighters were sortied in two waves, and they destroyed three Bf 110s for no loss. White and Allen attacked Hpt Willem Dorman's Bf 110G-4 of 3./NJG 1 near Groningen which blew up, although Dorman survived, injured. Wg Cdr Braham and Flt Lt Jacobs shot down two more Bf 110s near Schiermonikoog, both of which were flown by successful *Nachtjagd experten*. Ofw Georg Kraft (14 victories) was killed and 54-victory *experte* Fw Heinz Vinke survived, although his crew did not. Braham vividly recorded the action in his combat report;

'We flew to a point north of Schiermonikoog and then turned northeast. We continued on course for about five minutes when we sighted one Me 110 flying east and jinking. We turned and followed him towards the coast, closing in on the aircraft until we were at 300 yards range, 20 degrees starboard astern and a little below. Fire was opened with a two-second burst from all guns, and strikes were seen all over the enemy aircraft. Smoke came from the port engine and the Me 110 dived to port. We gave him another two-second burst from 250 yards and he caught fire and dived into the sea, burning on the water.

'Immediately afterwards we saw a second Me 110, which had been chasing us, a little above and turning gently to starboard on an easterly course. We gave a one second burst of cannon and machine gun at 50 yards in a gentle turn. The enemy aircraft appeared to blow up and we had to pull up and turn to port to avoid ramming it. At that point we saw one man bale out and his parachute open, and the enemy aircraft dived vertically into the sea in flames.'

In August, No 141 Sqn received its first Mosquito, and on the night of 6/7 September Harry White, flying Beaufighter VIF V8713, destroyed a

Ju 88 near Rheims. This proved to be the unit's final kill of the bomber support trial, during which it had flown some 233 sorties and claimed 13 enemy nightfighters destroyed for only three losses. These successes had been achieved in spite of the many limitations of the Beaufighter, and its radar. After analysis, the concept was deemed to have been successful, and for his leadership Braham received a well-deserved Bar to his DSO.

On 27/28 September Braham destroyed a Do 217 just west of Hanover to become the joint top-scoring nightfighter pilot with 20 kills. He went one better on the night of 29/30 September when, on a sortie over the Zuider Zee, he brought down the Bf 110 of NJG 1 53-victory *experte* Hpt August Geiger. These were his final Beaufighter claims. On 1 October Braham was replaced and sent to the Army Staff College at Camberley.

The Mosquito was by now very much in the ascendant, although some Beaufighter units remained. They included No 68 Sqn and Canadian-manned No 406 Sqn, led by Wg Cdr 'Moose' Fumerton, whose Beaufighter tally had reached 13 by the end of August 1943.

On 21 January 1944 there was an upsurge in activity when the so-called mini-*blitz* began with a 447-aircraft raid on London. But the level of activity was not sustained – 285 sorties on 29 January, 240 on 3 February and 200 on 18 and 20 February. Several new enemy types were encountered, including the He 177. One of those to encounter Heinkel's heavy bomber was future ace Sqn Ldr D J 'Blackie' Williams of No 406 Sqn, who was on patrol over the Channel on the night of 19 March 1944. The unit record book described what happened next;

'Contact was made 20 miles off Guernsey, and obtaining a visual on an enemy aircraft at 600 ft, the pilot identified it as a He 177. He shot it down into the sea from close range, both engines exploding.'

Two months later, on 14/15 May, No 68 Sqn's Miroslav Mansfeld destroyed two Do 217s. These represented his final claims, which took his total to eight and two shared kills. But the last victory by an ace in the UK came on the night

During the autumn of 1943 No 96 Sqn maintained a detachment at Drem, where Beaufighter VIF V8748/ZJ-R is seen being re-armed by WAAFs. The CO at the time was notable ace Wg Cdr Edward Crew, who flew this particular aircraft regularly on operations throughout the late summer, the first time being on 27 August 1943 (*late E D Crew*)

By late 1943 No 406 Sqn was commanded by the most successful RCAF nightfighter pilot of World War 2, Wg Cdr 'Moose' Fumerton. Based at Exeter for patrols over the Channel, one of its aircraft was KW103/HU-T, which was often flown by Fumerton, starting in late November (*M D Howley*)

The most prolific Czech pilot with No 68 Sqn was Sqn Ldr Miro Mansfeld (left), who is seen here with Flg Off Janacek standing in front of Beaufighter VIF ND211/WM-K at Fairwood Common on 15 May 1944. The previous night they had destroyed two Do 217s in this machine, and these proved to be Mansfeld's final victories against manned aircraft (*Zdenek Hurt*)

of 25 October. Moonlight was slanting through scattered cloud as seven-kill Mosquito ace Flg Off Desmond Tull of the elite Fighter Interception Unit patrolled at 2000 ft over the North Sea 60 miles east of Yarmouth under control of Hopton GCI. He reported;

'We were given trade five miles ahead on a vector of 160. Almost immediately we established contact 20 degrees to starboard, range 3.5 miles. We followed and closed to 2500 ft, where I visually established and identified the target as a He 111. I pulled up dead astern at a range of 250 yards and a height of 700 ft and fired a three-second burst. Strikes were seen and a shower of debris came back, followed by an opening parachute. The target was clearly illuminated by a concentration of red sparks, apparently caused by an explosion in the aircraft. I fired another burst of approximately four seconds. Strikes were seen and the target fell away to port into a violent spin. It hit the sea at 1945 hrs.'

Tull's only Beaufighter victory marked the end of the type's successful employment as a nightfighter defending British skies.

The final victory claimed by a Beaufighter ace in the UK was that scored by Flg Off Desmond Tull of the elite Fighter Interception Unit, to which this Mk VIF V8565/ZQ-F belonged. Tull's victim was an He 111H-20 V1 missile carrier (*P H T Green Collection*)

COASTAL FIGHTERS

The Beaufighter was also considered to be useful in the long-range fighter role to Coastal Command. With the Focke-Wulf Fw 200 Condor posing

The first Beaufighter to be delivered to a coastal fighter squadron was R2198/PN-B, which was issued to No 252 Sqn at Chivenor on 27 December 1940, although it was not fitted to full Mk IC standard and was therefore used for training only (*Bristol*)

This poor but nevertheless interesting photograph, taken 'over the fence' at Aldergrove, shows one of No 252 Sqn's Beaufighters on detachment in April 1941. Because the individual letter is partially obscured, it is uncertain if it is PN-H or PN-K. If the latter, then it is T3237, which was the aircraft that Flt Lt Bill Riley used to shoot down a Fw 200 Condor on 16 April to record the squadron's first victory (*D H Newton*)

a significant threat to Britain's vital shipping, this received top priority. Eventually, the Beaufighter was deployed on anti-shipping strikes, although it was also used in the pure long-range anti-aircraft fighter role. A number of pilots were successful, and several became aces at a time when encounters with the Luftwaffe were relatively rare.

The first coastal fighter unit to receive the Beaufighter was No 252 Sqn, based at Chivenor, in Devon. Its first aircraft arrived for training on 27 December 1940, and it collected its first fully-equipped Mk IC (R2152) from St Athan on New Year's Day. Norfolk-based No 235 Sqn also received a few for use alongside its Blenheim IVs, although the unit was not to get its full complement for another year.

At the end of the month Flt Lt Bill Riley, who had gained several successes the previous year, was posted to No 252 Sqn from No 608 Sqn. The unit continued to train, and on 4 April 1941 'A' Flight moved to Aldergrove, in Northern Ireland, where it became operational as part of No 15 Group Coastal Command. But the weather was poor and flights were restricted, although the unit mounted grid searches for enemy aircraft in the North-Western Approaches. On one, on the 16th, Bill Riley, with Wt Off Donaldson, (in T3237/PN-K) destroyed a Fw 200 off Scotland. It was his sixth kill. Riley described the squadron's first success;

'At the end of the patrol an enemy aircraft was sighted at 1420 hrs on a course of 210 degrees. Identified as a Condor. I started my attack from the beam to quarter, finishing up astern. Fire was opened at 300 yards and continued in short bursts to point blank range when astern. The Condor replied with the midship gun. The Condor caught fire at the rear port wing root, both engines appearing unserviceable. The Condor swung to the left, straightened out, then dived into the sea in flames at an angle of 45 degrees. No survivors, and very little wreckage were seen. The Condor was painted entirely green, with crosses silhouetted in white. No lower gondola observed.'

33

Riley's victim was Fw 200C-3 Wk-Nr 0039 (F8+AH) of 1./KG 40, and Oblt Hermann Richter and his crew were lost. After a few more patrols the squadron prepared to detach to Malta for approximately a month. The ten aircraft departed England on 29 April 1941.

Coastal fighter unit No 272 Sqn began its conversion at around this time, but on 24 May it too was ordered to move to the Middle East. The element that remained in Britain was absorbed by No 143 Sqn during June. The following month another Blenheim unit, No 248 Sqn at Bircham Newton, began re-equipping. In August, the unit's Sqn Ldr David Cartridge flew his first operation. He would end the war as a leading coastal fighter pilot, with two kills and three shared to his credit.

On Christmas Eve, after a hurried conversion, and led by its CO, Wg Cdr Hugh Garlick, No 235 Sqn flew to Sumburgh for its first major operation. Its Beaufighters were to provide fighter cover for the Commando raid on Vaagso, on the Norwegian coast, on 27 December 1941. There were several brushes with Bf 109s, some of which were chased off, although one aircraft was shot down. No 248 was also involved, and David Cartridge began his progress to ace status when he downed a He 111 near Vaagso. It was one of two which fell to the unit.

Both squadrons remained in Scotland during early 1942, maintaining patrols over the North Sea. In May No 235 Sqn moved to Norfolk and then on to Chivenor in July for patrols over the Bay of Biscay. During August its crews found some success by downing three Arado Ar 196 floatplanes over the Bay and also damaged two Fw 200s. The following month the unit claimed five Ju 88s and an Fw 200 destroyed over Biscay.

Further north, No 248 Sqn's patrols occasionally found enemy flying boats. On 4 July Australian Sgt Ron Hammond opened his account when he forced a Blohm und Voss Bv 138 to land in the sea off Goosen Island. During the summer No 248 Sqn was ordered to send a large detachment to Malta in support of Operation *Pedestal*. It later returned to Pembrokeshire and flew fighter patrols over the Western Approaches and Biscay in support of Coastal Command's anti-submarine aircraft.

Flying from Talbenny, on 25 September Hammond damaged a Ju 88 off Brest, and on 13 October he shot down another in concert with Sqn Ldr Cartridge and Flt Lt Melville-Jackson. Hammond also downed an unidentified seaplane (probably an Ar 196) that same day. On 29 November a squadron patrol led by Flt Lt Aubrey Inniss found six Ju 88s

In December 1941 No 235 Sqn was hurriedly converted onto the Beaufighter IC in time to participate in the Vaagso raid, during which it encountered Bf 109s and lost one aircraft to them. Three days later at Dyce, T4725/LA-J (flown by Sgt Denley) taxied into LA-O and a Hudson before Sgt Cummins in T3295/LA-S ran into the lot! The resulting devastation was shown in the squadron's line book (*No 235 Sqn records*)

On 13 October 1942 future Coastal Command ace Flt Lt George Melville-Jackson was on a fighter sweep when he shot down a Ju 88 for his second victory. But as he recorded in his logbook, 'Own aircraft hit by return fire in nose and port wing. Hole 2 ft square between starboard engine and fuselage caused by bits flying off Ju 88' (*G H Melville-Jackson*)

attacking a lone Armstrong Whitworth Whitley over the Bay. Engaging the German aircraft, he claimed one probable, while Ron Hammond damaged another. Three days later the Australian was attacked by Fw 190s during a patrol and was killed. His DFM award was gazetted soon afterwards.

Inniss was involved again on 29 January 1943 when his patrol spotted two Ju 88s. The leading pair shot down the first, and while this action was in progress, Inniss (in WR-B) engaged the second. The unit's record book said of the action;

'"B" registered hits with a long burst of cannon fire and the enemy aircraft was seen to crash into the water burning furiously then appeared to disintegrate into burning patches.'

The squadron found more action over Biscay on 9 February when a line patrol led by David Cartridge, with Flt Lt Melville-Jackson and Plt Off White, encountered four Ju 88 long-range fighters. A dogfight began, during which the Junkers formed a defensive circle before individual combats broke out. Two fell to the Beaufighters, while another, attacking head-on, was hit and its port engine fell away. The Ju 88 ditched. All three were credited with three shared victories, taking both Cartridge and Melville-Jackson to ace status. The latter described Cartridge to the author as 'a superb pilot, quite fearless and a magnificent leader in the air'.

Aubrey Inniss was in action again on 10 March, leading a routine line patrol. Over Biscay, he spotted a Ju 88 and climbed to attack. The squadron record book again takes up the story;

'The enemy aircraft sighted our Beaufighters when Inniss was 1000 yards behind. The enemy aircraft reached cloud after he had fired a burst with cannon, but these then failed owing to a fault. Stringer then closed in as the enemy aircraft flew in a thin cloud, giving it a burst of machine gun fire and observing hits on the port tailplane. He then broke away as Maurice came into attack. He fired a two-second burst from 300 yards range astern, hits registered on engines and cockpit. He then closed to 150 yards dead astern, level with the enemy aircraft, and fired a two-second burst resulting in the enemy aircraft bursting into flames immediately. The Ju 88 banked steeply to port, the whole aircraft being ablaze, and straightened up and glided towards the sea, before crashing into the water. During the combat, aircraft "W" was seriously damaged, and although well-nigh uncontrollable, he succeeded in reaching base and made a crash landing.'

This was thought to have been Inniss' final success, some sources crediting him with as many as eight victories.

Coastal Beaufighter units maintained patrols with occasional success, No 404 Sqn RCAF, for example, downing four Bv 138s on 28 July while supporting the Home Fleet. However, there were fewer opportunities for pilots to build large scores, especially as the 'fighter' task decreased with units concentrating on the anti-shipping role.

1
Beaufighter IF R2069/ZK-H of Plt Off M J Herrick, No 25 Sqn, Wittering, March 1941

2
Beaufighter IF V8324/RO-B of Plt Off R J L Mellersh, No 29 Sqn, West Malling, August-September 1942

3
Beaufighter VIF ND243/Q of Wt Off R T Butler, No 46 Sqn, Gambut, Libya, September-October 1944

4
Beaufighter IF X7583/WM-E of Wt Off L Bobek,
No 68 Sqn, Coltishall, 28 April 1942

5
Beaufighter VIF ND211/WM-K of Sqn Ldr M J
Mansfeld, No 68 Sqn, Fairwood Common,
14 May 1944

6
Beaufighter IF X7671/WP-D of Sqn Ldr D S Pain,
No 89 Sqn, Abu Sueir, Egypt, 2/3 March 1942

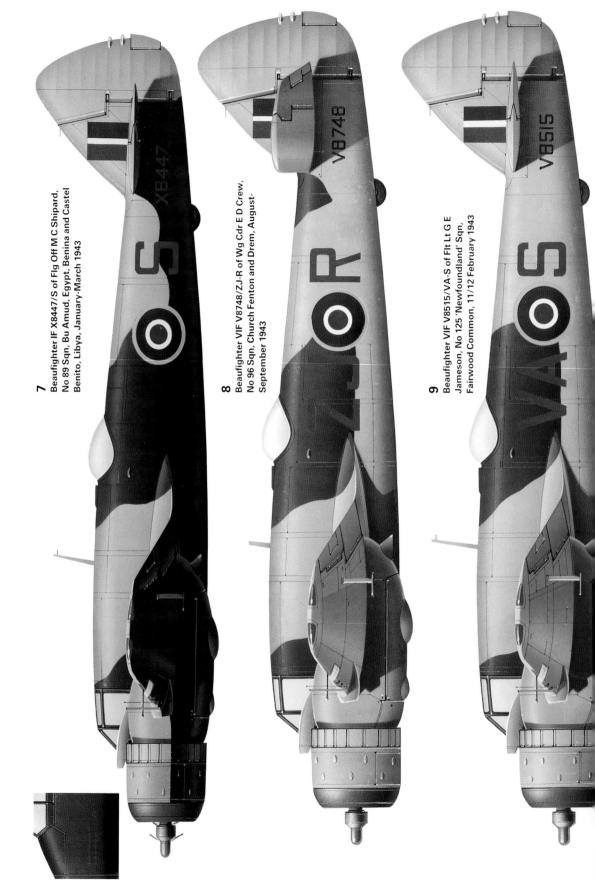

7
Beaufighter IF X8447/S of Flg Off M C Shipard,
No 89 Sqn, Bu Amud, Egypt, Benina and Castel
Benito, Libya, January-March 1943

8
Beaufighter VIF V8748/ZJ-R of Wg Cdr E D Crew,
No 96 Sqn, Church Fenton and Drem, August-
September 1943

9
Beaufighter VIF V8515/VA-S of Flt Lt G E
Jameson, No 125 'Newfoundland' Sqn,
Fairwood Common, 11/12 February 1943

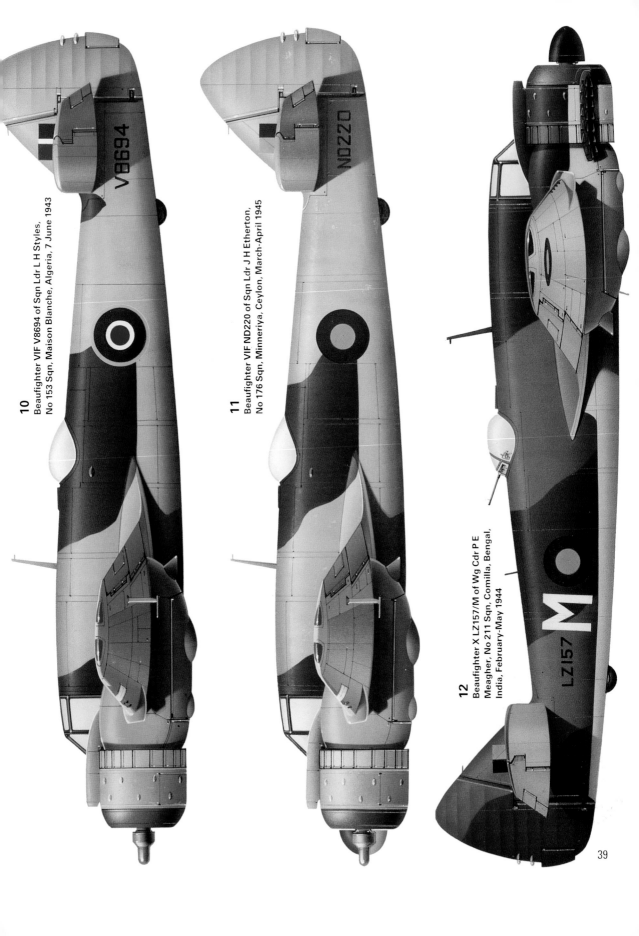

10
Beaufighter VIF V8694 of Sqn Ldr L H Styles,
No 153 Sqn, Maison Blanche, Algeria, 7 June 1943

11
Beaufighter VIF ND220 of Sqn Ldr J H Etherton,
No 176 Sqn, Minneriya, Ceylon, March-April 1945

12
Beaufighter X LZ157/M of Wg Cdr P E
Meagher, No 211 Sqn, Comilla, Bengal,
India, February-May 1944

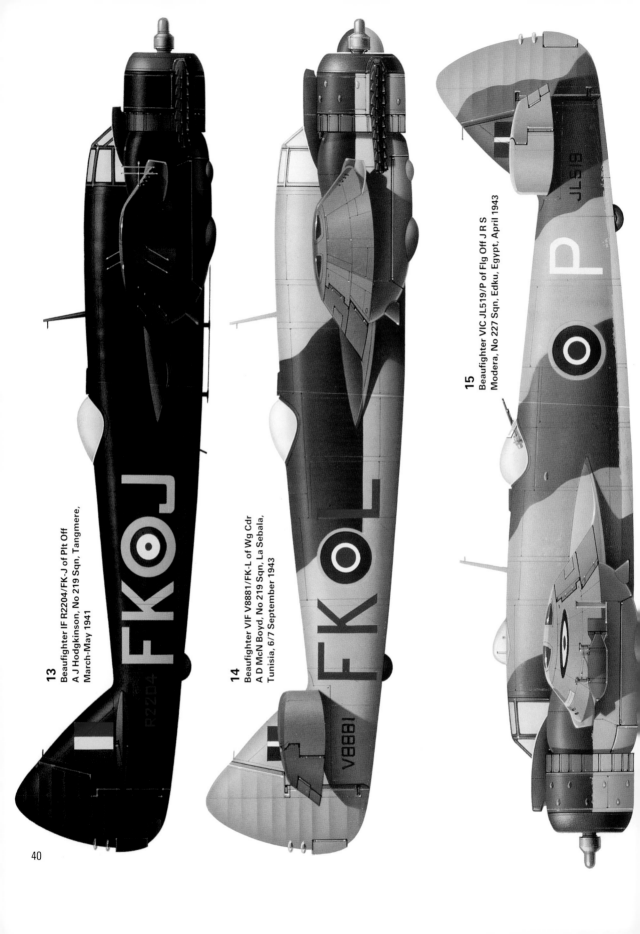

13
Beaufighter IF R2204/FK-J of Plt Off
A J Hodgkinson, No 219 Sqn, Tangmere,
March-May 1941

14
Beaufighter VIF V8881/FK-L of Wg Cdr
A D McN Boyd, No 219 Sqn, La Sebala,
Tunisia, 6/7 September 1943

15
Beaufighter VIC JL519/P of Flg Off J R S
Modera, No 227 Sqn, Edku, Egypt, April 1943

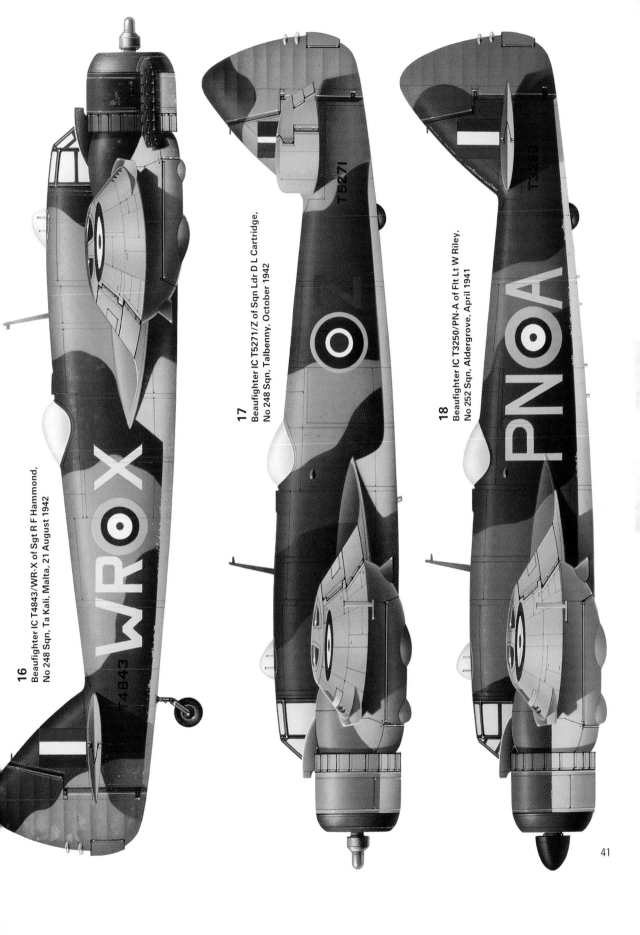

16
Beaufighter IC T4843/WR-X of Sgt R F Hammond,
No 248 Sqn, Ta Kali, Malta, 21 August 1942

17
Beaufighter IC T5271/Z of Sqn Ldr D L Cartridge,
No 248 Sqn, Talbenny, October 1942

18
Beaufighter IC T3250/PN-A of Flt Lt W Riley,
No 252 Sqn, Aldergrove, April 1941

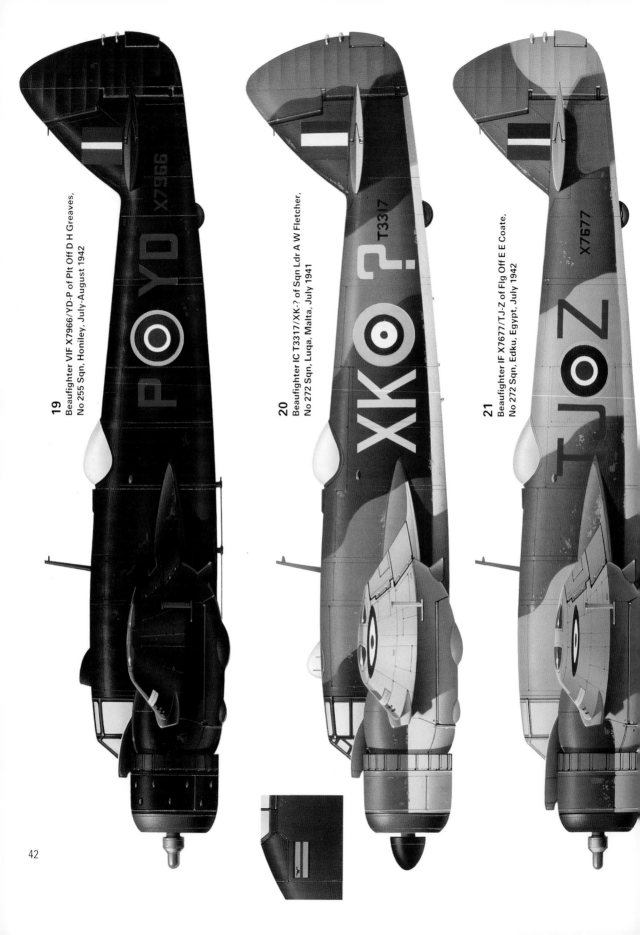

19
Beaufighter VIF X7966/YD-P of Plt Off D H Greaves,
No 255 Sqn, Honiley, July-August 1942

20
Beaufighter IC T3317/XK-? of Sqn Ldr A W Fletcher,
No 272 Sqn, Luqa, Malta, July 1941

21
Beaufighter IF X7677/TJ-Z of Flg Off E E Coate,
No 272 Sqn, Edku, Egypt, July 1942

22
Beaufighter VIF KW103/HU-T of Wg Cdr
R C Fumerton , No 406 Sqn RCAF, Exeter,
27 November 1943

23
Beaufighter IIF T3145/KP-K of Sqn Ldr
R M Trousdale, No 409 Sqn RCAF,
Coleby Grange, 3 March 1942

24
Beaufighter IIF T3017/RX-B of Wg Cdr C G C
Olive, No 456 Sqn RAAF, Valley, December 1941

43

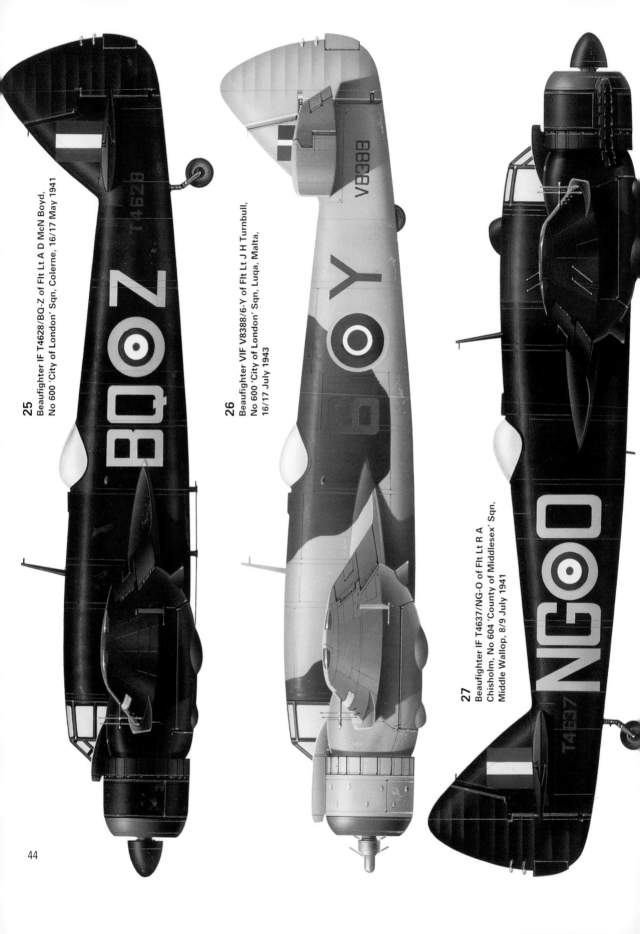

25
Beaufighter IF T4628/BQ-Z of Flt Lt A D McN Boyd,
No 600 'City of London' Sqn, Colerne, 16/17 May 1941

26
Beaufighter VIF V8388/6-Y of Flt Lt J H Turnbull,
No 600 'City of London' Sqn, Luqa, Malta,
16/17 July 1943

27
Beaufighter IF T4637/NG-O of Flt Lt R A
Chisholm, No 604 'County of Middlesex' Sqn,
Middle Wallop, 8/9 July 1941

28
Beaufighter VIF MM856/NG-C of Wg Cdr M H
Constable-Maxwell, No 604 'County of
Middlesex' Sqn, Scorton, 23 August 1943

29
Beaufighter IF X7750/B of Flt Lt G L Hayton,
No 1435 Flt, Luqa, Malta, March 1942

30
Beaufighter IC A19-40/EH-G of Sqn Ldr R L
Gordon, No 31 Sqn RAAF, Coomalie Creek,
Northern Territory, Australia, 9 October 1943

AROUND THE MEDITERRANEAN

The Beaufighter's range and firepower made it suitable for escort and strike duties in the Mediterranean. The first aircraft to be deployed in the theatre took the form of 13 No 252 Sqn Mk ICs sent to Malta on detachment in early May 1941. There, they provided long-range fighter escort to the fast merchantman SS *Parracombe*, which was carrying crated Hurricanes from Gibraltar. A convoy of escorting ships was also sent from Egypt, but the *Parracombe* struck a mine off Cap Bon and foundered.

Despite life being grim on Malta, the squadron drew its first blood escorting Blenheim IVs off Lampedusa on 7 May when Detachment CO Sqn Ldr Yaxley, Sub Lt Fraser and Bill Riley downed an Italian Savoia-Marchetti SM.81 transport. On 10 May the Beaufighters mounted strafing attacks on Sicilian airfields, with several aircraft being damaged at Catania and two destroyed and five damaged at Comiso.

Six days later eight Beaufighters hastily deployed to Maleme, on the island of Crete, and on the morning of the 17th they attacked German-held airfields in southern Greece, causing considerable damage. This did little to halt the coming invasion, however, and the detachment's surviving elements left Malta a few days later. Four escorted Hurricanes to Egypt and four returned to England. Bill Riley remained in hospital in Malta, having been injured by a Hurricane in a case of mistaken identity. On the 23rd two Beaufighters, led by Yaxley, sortied from Egypt and strafed Maleme, which was now in enemy hands. They claimed eight Ju 52/3ms destroyed, but it was to little avail.

By then No 272 Sqn, also recently re-equipped with Beaufighters, had been ordered to Edku, in Egypt. From there on 1 June Sqn Ldr A W Fletcher flew its first sortie. The unit was mainly involved with covering shipping evacuating troops from Crete. No 272 Sqn also participated in

During July 1941 a detachment of aircraft from No 272 Sqn moved to Malta, led by the CO, Sqn Ldr A W Fletcher. Although he did not achieve any aerial victories, he destroyed nine enemy aircraft during two well-executed airfield attacks at the end of the month. Fletcher flew this particular aircraft from Malta on a number of occasions (*British Official*)

Sqn Ldr Fletcher poses with Beaufighter IC T3317/XK-? during his time on Malta. The '?' and his rank pennant were a privilege of his position as squadron CO (*J A Heath*)

the invasion of Syria in June, beginning with an attack on oil installations in Beirut flown from Lydda, in Palestine. In Egypt, the under-strength elements of both squadrons were concentrated into one, while Sqn Ldr Fletcher of No 272 Sqn led eight to Malta to join others flown in from England. The Beaufighters were soon in action.

On 24 June they made the squadron's first combat claims when Flt Lt Campbell shot down two Ju 87s during a convoy escort. This was followed by strafing attacks on Sicilian airfields when Fletcher, in his personally-marked T3317/XK-?, attacked Borizzo airfield, near Marsala, destroying four SM.79s and two CR.42s. Flg Off Clarke increased the squadron's 'bag' by shooting down a Cant Z.501 floatplane, while other aircraft were hit at Catania. Two days later Fletcher strafed Cagliari airfield, on Sardinia, destroying three more SM.79s. In early August the detachment returned to Egypt.

DESERT HUNTERS

No 89 Sqn was formed at Colerne in September 1941 with AI-equipped Beaufighter IFs. The first nightfighter unit to be despatched overseas, it left for Egypt in late November, and by 10 December was established at Abu Sueir for the night defence of the vital Suez Canal area. There, many of its all-black aircraft had their top surfaces over-painted in desert camouflage, with the undersides remaining black. By the time No 89 Sqn arrived, Nos 252 and 272 Sqns had become fully independent again.

On 18 November Operation *Crusader* began with the objective of relieving Tobruk. With heavy rain having rendered the German airfields near Gazala inoperable, No 272 Sqn's first victories of the campaign were over two Tmimi-based Ju 52/3ms, which were shot down. An attack on the transports' airfield that afternoon found five more just taking off, and all of them were downed, together with a passing Hs 126 and a Fi 156.

Beaufighter IC T3250/A of No 252 Sqn was one of the aircraft the unit took to the Middle East in 1941. It became part of the joint unit with No 272 Sqn, hence the over-painting of its code letters. In the UK, it had been flown on several occasions by ace Flt Lt Bill Riley (*G S Leslie*)

Two days later, again over Tmimi, Plt Off Walters, with Sgts Price and Ross, downed four Ju 87s and a Fi 156 between them. The pace was maintained over the following days, with long range attacks and escorts being the main task. Both units were fully engaged as heavy fighting raged on the ground and occasional losses were suffered.

Tobruk was relieved in December, and it was while escorting a

convoy on 18 January 1942 that one of No 252 Sqn's new pilots began to make his mark. During one attack, Plt Off Herbert Gunnis, flying T4834/BT-F, shot down a Ju 88 and probably destroyed two more on his way to becoming an ace. The following day there was an Axis counterattack, and the weakened Allies fell back. Benghazi was lost, but the line stabilised during February.

At Edku, after a long wait, No 89 Sqn finally enjoyed success on the night of 2 March when Sqn Ldr Derek Pain shot down a He 111 for the RAF's first radar-controlled victory over Egypt. The second was not long in coming, for Flg Off 'Moose' Fumerton downed another, although he was slightly wounded by return fire. No 89 Sqn's unique capabilities meant that it soon had detachments operating throughout the area. Its successes grew so that by the end of the war it was to rank as the RAF's second highest-scoring nightfighter squadron with 141.3 victories (No 600 Sqn was the most successful with 180 kills).

Both the attack squadrons continued to have occasional air combat successes too. One came on 11 March when Gunnis was escorting a Tobruk convoy, which was attacked by six enemy bombers. In a very one-sided fight he shot down two He 111s and a Ju 88. Flg Off A D Frecker also brought down two He 111s and future ace Canadian Plt Off Albert Smith accounted for a Ju 88 to score his first victory.

It was while escorting torpedo bombers attacking a convoy heading for Tripoli a month later that Sqn Ldr Bill Riley – now with No 272 Sqn – claimed again – two Bf 110s (one was actually a Do 17Z), which were escorting the ships. These victories made him an ace.

Beaufighter IC T3246/J was flown by No 252 Sqn when it was operating from Edku under the umbrella of No 272 Sqn during late 1941. It could cope well with the rugged desert conditions - perhaps even better than the crew transport! (*J Pelly-Fry*)

Also seen at Edku in mid-1941 is T3316/M of No 272 Sqn, which, among other things, was involved in operations against Syria when flown by Belgian pilot Sgt le Jeune. He flew several sorties over Turkish waters while searching for a Vichy French tanker (*Bristol*)

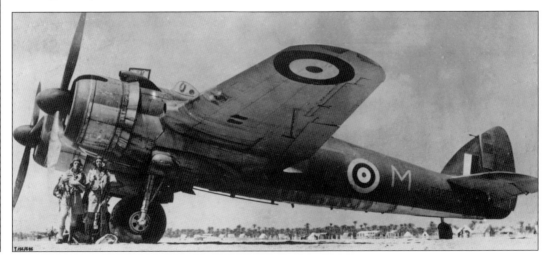

The Beaufighter IFs of No 89 Sqn only wore their WP identification letters for a short time, as illustrated here by X7671/WP-D at Abu Sueir in spring 1942. Sqn Ldr Derek Pain shot down a He 111 while flying it on the night of 2/3 March to claim the squadron's long-awaited first victory, and his second. He later became an ace, while No 89 Sqn ended up becoming one of the top-scoring nightfighter units (*via author*)

Beaufighter IC T4882/TJ-Z, displaying No 272 Sqn's little-used TJ codes, looks rather sad after a heavy landing at Edku on 25 March 1942. Twelve days earlier it had been used by one of the squadron's more successful pilots, Flg Off D H Hammond, to damage a SM.79 off Tobruk (*R A Butt*)

Flg Off Derek Hammond of No 272 Sqn is carried on the shoulders of his colleagues after the award of his DFC on 7 April 1942 (*late D H Hammond*)

The port of Alexandria and the Suez Canal were major targets for the enemy, and on 28/29 April No 89 Sqn's Edku element engaged 25 I./LG 1 Ju 88s and 5./KG 100 He 111s raiding the port. Sqn Ldr J A A 'Jasper' Read brought down both a Ju 88 and a He 111 and Kiwi Flt Lt 'Rusty' Mackenzie achieved a probable. Both were to become aces. The detachment brought down another Ju 88 two nights later.

On the night of 11 May Plt Off Michael Kinmonth was vectored onto several contacts and shot down an SM.79 – the first of his seven victories over the coming year – and damaged a second. Three days earlier No 46 Sqn had become the second Egyptian-based nightfighter unit when it began reforming at Edku from No 89 Sqn's detachment, thus expanding the area's nightfighting capability. It was initially commanded by Sqn Ldr 'Jasper' Read, who had recently made his first claims.

It had become apparent that the Luftwaffe was flying a large number of reinforcements to Rommel between Crete and Libya, and an attempt was made to intercept them on the morning of 12 May. Patrolling off the North African coast, six of No 252 Sqn's Beaufighters, escorted by Kittyhawks from No 250 Sqn, encountered 13 Ju 52/3ms each carrying 20 troops, and escorted by just two Bf 110s. It was a one-sided fight, and a contemporary account describes Herbert Gunnis' part in it;

'On the R/T, as "Bandit. Tally Ho! Ten o'clock" was called, he pulled up above the leader and sighted a large formation of three-engined enemy transports, escorted by at least two Me 110s. These were about two miles ahead and five degrees to port. Plt Off Gunnis opened fire at 300 yards range, closing to 50, with two long bursts of cannon and machine gun fire. He then broke away to port, turned around and observed one Ju 52 burst into flames. He carried on a circuit and made a further head-on attack, observing a Ju 52 on the port side burst into flames and fall into the water dead ahead.'

Beaufighter IC T4831/BT-D of No 252
Sqn took part in the notable action
of 12 May 1942 when six
Beaufighters and their Kittyhawk
escorts attacked an escorted
formation of Ju 52/3ms over the
Mediterranean. During the action Plt
Off Gunnis became the squadron's
latest ace, while Flt Sgt Reginald
Ivey despatched two of the
transports while flying this aircraft
(*via G R Pitchfork*)

But Gunnis' hydraulics had been hit by return fire early in the action, necessitating a wheels-up landing back at base. He was credited with one destroyed and one damaged to become an ace. Two weeks later the relative stalemate in the desert ended when Rommel began an all-out attack on the Gazala-Bir Hacheim line. It was to be the precursor to heavy air fighting over both the desert and Mediterranean convoy routes.

BATTLE FOR MALTA

Malta had been under siege for over a year, but remained a constant threat to the Axis campaign in North Africa. In early 1942 the island was subjected to a sustained effort to neutralise it. On 8 March the defences were reinforced by four Beaufighter IFs of No 89 Sqn, which flew into Ta Kali where they were initially attached to No 1435 Flt. Among the four pilots were three who were soon to make names for themselves – Flt Lt Gil Hayton (in X7750/B), Plt Off E G Daniel (in X7648) and Sgt R A Miller (in X7586). They were soon in action.

In the early evening of the 12th Hayton and his navigator Flg Off Norman Josling were scrambled to intercept bombers, and severely damaged one (possible a Ju 88). But 'Dusty' Miller went one better and claimed the detachment's first confirmed kill by downing a Ju 88C nightfighter (R4+V8 of I./NJG 2) flown by Oblt Schulz and crew, who were killed. They then damaged a He 111. It was a successful start.

The detachment continued to be held on standby so that it built up a stream of successes, despite the dangers and privations of life on Malta. One came in the early hours of 12 April when bombs again began falling. Miller and Sgt Tearle found a BR.20M over Gozo and sent it down in flames. Miller later spoke to one of the survivors, a gunner, who described the Beaufighter's shells slamming into the aircraft and the pilot asking if he was testing his guns, moments before the port engine burst into flames!

There were more raids two nights later. At 2030 hrs Plt Off 'Tubby' Daniel's navigator, Sgt Gosling, vectored them onto a Fiat BR20 flown

by Ten Ceccato. After a long chase, he managed to hit it just south of Sicily, and the blazing aircraft came down near Scoglitti. Almost a month later, in the early hours of 17 May, eight BR.20Ms from 88° *Gruppo* approached Malta. Daniel and Gosling engaged three, all of which they claimed shot down, although one might have been a Ju 88. These three claims made Daniel No 89 Sqn's first ace. 'Tubby' Daniel was quite a character, and he was often seen during the day delivering equipment and refreshments to the groundcrew with the pony and trap he had acquired.

Malta's agony continued day and night, and by early June conditions were desperate, with supplies and munitions on the verge of running out. It was then decided to mount Operation *Harpoon* from Gibraltar, with another convoy coming from Alexandria.

On 10 June the Beaufighters of No 235 Sqn, under Wg Cdr Hugh Garlick, arrived from England on detachment for offensive and anti-shipping work. No 89 Sqn's aircraft remained active, with Miller (in V8224/F) shooting down a Ju 88 for his third victory the night No 235 Sqn arrived. Four days later, at the height of the *Harpoon* battle, Gil Hayton claimed one of the attacking Ju 88s for his fifth victory.

Just before midnight on the 17th a patrolling Beaufighter flown by 'Tubby' Daniel was vectored onto a Ju 88 intruder, which was shot down to became his seventh, and final, victim. Hayton claimed another Ju 88 (his last), while Flg Off P G Oakes destroyed a Junkers bomber the following night. This was the detachment's final claim, for it departed for Egypt the next day. Some 18.5 kills had been claimed, six by Hayton, seven by Daniel and four by newly promoted Plt Off Miller. All received DFCs, and Miller reached ace status in 1944 flying Mosquitos.

On 22 June four replacement aircraft and six crews from 'C' Flight, under Flt Lt Henry Edwards, arrived. So too had four future aces – Edwards himself, Flg Off 'Moose' Fumerton, who already had four victories, Flg Off Mervyn Shipard (one) and Plt Off Nevil Reeves. They were soon in action. Just before midnight on the 23rd, Edwards and Sgt J R Phillipson downed a Ju 88 into the sea north of Malta. The following night Fumerton became an ace when (in Z7716/A) he found a Ju 87 dive-bomber, which was despatched. They were airborne again just before dawn and his fire downed a Cant Z.1007bis.

Fumerton and Bing claimed two Ju 88s three nights later, and two more on successive nights at the beginning of July. 2/3 July also saw Reeves, with Sgt A A O'Leary, claim the first of his eventual 14 victories.

No 89 Sqn Beaufighter IF X7750/B was one of the aircraft detached to Malta in early March 1942, where it was used by Flt Lt Gil Hayton to make all of his claims over the next three months. The first was for an aircraft damaged on the night of 12 March, and a week later he shot down a Fiat BR.20M for the first of his five or six victories. It was also used by Plt Off 'Tubby' Daniel to claim his first victory during April. The men in the picture are thought to be Hayton (left) and his navigator, Flg Off Norman Josling (*Frank Wingham Collection*)

He was also airborne on the night of the 30th when four KGr 806 Ju 88s raided the island. West of Gozo, Oblt Hermann's M7+FK was intercepted by Reeves, who sent it crashing into the sea for his fourth confirmed victory.

In spite of the June convoy the supply situation remained fragile. A massive new convoy was planned for mid-August as Malta faced starvation. In preparation for Operation *Pedestal,* on the 7th the first Beaufighter fitted with AI Mk VII radar arrived at the same time as No 248 Sqn's strike Beaufighters flew out from England. Among the unit's pilots were future aces Sqn Ldr David Cartridge and Flt Lt George Melville-Jackson. The squadron was soon hitting enemy airfields.

Two of the more successful pilots serving with No 248 Sqn's Malta detachment in 1942 were Sqn Ldr David Cartridge (left) and Flt Lt George Melville-Jackson, who each ended the war with two and three shared victories
(*G H Melville-Jackson*)

The *Pedestal* battle was one of the defining moments of the war in the Mediterranean, for the incoming supplies were just enough to keep the island going. When the crippled tanker *Ohio* docked on 15 August the enemy redoubled its efforts to destroy the vessel. That night 15 Italian bombers set out, although most turned back. One that did not was Ten Col Ravazzoni's SM.84 MM24564, which was intercepted by Nevil Reeves. He wrote of his fifth successful combat;

'At approximately 2200 hrs exhausts of an enemy aircraft were seen going south. It turned north and we closed to 100 yards and fired. The port engine of the enemy aircraft caught fire immediately and numerous pieces fell off. I skidded the aircraft over and shot at the starboard engine. The whole aircraft was enveloped in fire and went into the sea, where it burned for ten minutes.'

'Moose' Fumerton was also up, and he destroyed a Z.1007 for his 12th night victory. Aircraft from Nos 235 and 248 Sqns were active too. During the afternoon of the 21st, the latter unit escorted a strike on a convoy off Paxos. Promptly wading into the escort, Sgt Ron Hammond (in T4843/WR-X) reported;

'I sighted a Ju 88 about 500 ft above us and approximately 1000 yards away, travelling north. I climbed and opened fire, closing in to 150 yards,

To support the vital *Pedestal* convoy in August 1942, No 248 Sqn was detached to Malta, from where several of its more notable pilots made their claims. One was Sgt Ron Hammond, who, on 21 August flew T4843/WR-X (the aircraft furthest from the camera in this formation) escorting a convoy attack off Paxos. Having probably destroyed a Ju 88 during the sortie, he then 'noticed a Piaggio P.32 (probably a BR.20 – Editor) at about 1000 ft. We climbed after this and approached him at about 2400 ft, opening fire at his starboard quarter from about 400 yards. Hits were observed on his starboard engine, which burst into flames immediately. He then turned slowly to port and we delivered a third attack. We shot away his port tailfin – large pieces just missing our aircraft – and hits were observed along his fuselage and starboard wing. Oil covered our windscreen, and he was observed spinning out of control at about 50-100 ft'
(*G H Melville-Jackson*)

and when breaking away I noticed voluminous white smoke coming from the starboard engine. We then manoeuvred into position and delivered an attack from dead astern. Flames were observed coming from its starboard engine and we opened fire again at 300 yards. More hits were observed along the fuselage and starboard mainplane. We closed to 50 yards and pulled up sharply 100 ft from the water. When last seen, the Ju 88 was in a slight dive, with its starboard wing down.

'As we pulled away from the attack on the Ju 88, we noticed a (Piaggio) P.32 at about 1000 ft. We climbed after it and approached at about 2400 ft, opening fire from its starboard quarter from about 400 yards. Hits were observed on the aircraft's starboard engine, which burst into flames immediately. It then turned slowly to port and we manoeuvred into position and delivered a second attack from the port quarter. No hits were observed and the aircraft turned inside us. We throttled back, manoeuvred into position dead astern and delivered a third attack. We shot away the port tailfin – large pieces just missing our aircraft – and hits were observed along the fuselage and starboard wing. Oil covered our windscreen, and the P.32 spun out of control at about 50-100 ft.'

Another pilot involved was George Melville-Jackson, who recalled;

'I sighted two enemy aircraft at about 500 ft above us. I climbed and attacked the second one. I started firing at about 400 yards and closed to 100 yards dead astern, at which time I noticed pieces coming off the starboard engine. As I broke away, the aircraft dived straight into the sea.'

But his Beaufighter was also damaged during the engagement and it crash-landed at Luqa, where No 227 Sqn had recently formed from the No 235 Sqn detachment. It was immediately in action, and included a newly arrived 20-year-old Canadian who would soon make his mark in Malta – Plt Off Dallas Schmidt. Late on the afternoon of 27 August he was escorting Beauforts attacking a tanker off Crete. Schmidt spotted a Z.1007 ahead of him and quickly turned right to engage it and 'gave him a short burst and pieces fell off the fuselage and the tail fell off. The second burst set his starboard engine on fire and the third burst set his port engine on fire. The rear gunner of the Cant fired on us the whole time of the engagement. The aircraft was all ablaze when it crashed into the sea.' It was the first of his 8.5 victories.

The previous night, with nocturnal attacks now reduced, permission had been given for No 89 Sqn's Beaufighters (stripped of their radar) to fly over Sicilian airfields. Late on the 26th Flt Lt Henry Edwards flew the first raid, and over Marsala he saw an aircraft take off. He wrote on his return;

'I closed in behind it and with full flap managed to stay there. From very close range I gave it two short bursts. Bits came off the wings, tail and hull. It stalled to the right and crashed just south of Marsala in a blaze which lit up the whole town.'

Beaufighter VIC X8035/J of No 227 Sqn lifts off from Malta soon after the unit's formation on 20 August 1942. The squadron was heavily involved in attacks on enemy air and sea transport, and sustained quite heavy losses. This aircraft was to be lost on a strike on the MV *Delphi* on 27 August while being flown by Flt Sgt Eric O'Hara. It was during this mission that young Canadian Plt Off Dallas Schmidt shot down a Cant Z.1007 to begin his journey to ace status (*via J D Oughton*)

No 89 Sqn navigator Douglas Oxby was crewed with leading RAAF nightfighter ace Flg Off Mervyn Shipard, and they enjoyed great success over Malta and the desert. Returning to England, Oxby went on to enjoy a successful career with No 219 Sqn, and ended the war as the RAF's most successful nightfighter navigator with some 21 successful interceptions to his credit (*D Oxby*)

His fifth victory was claimed as a Do 18 flying boat. No 89 Sqn also began escorting Beauforts attacking convoys, and during one such mission on 6 September Nevil Reeves reported attacking Ju 88s;

'I saw a Ju 88 8-10 miles south of the convoy, squirted and saw bits fly off the port engine and starboard wing. I broke away as another Ju 88 was shooting from behind me to starboard. I turned 360 degrees and lost the attacker. I then looked for my previous Ju 88, which was near sea level, going slowly, with smoke pouring from both engines, heading for shore. Several single-engined fighters were above it, so I did not attack again.'

These were probably Macchi C.200s, as Henry Edwards reported;

'I saw three single-engined fighters approaching head on, slightly to port. I turned towards them and climbed. I attacked the nearest fighter, firing one long burst from quarter to beam. I saw bursts on the fighter before I passed over the top of it.'

Reeves was credited with a destroyed and Edwards a damaged. Other pilots also claimed kills, but two Beaufighters were lost in return.

In mid-October, just as a 'mini-*blitz*' on Malta began, No 227 Sqn received a new CO in the form of Wg Cdr Cedric Masterman. No 89 Sqn remained busy, and on the first night of the *blitz* Sgt Douggie Oxby guided Flg Off Mervyn Shipard to attack a lone He 111 over Luqa as it turned for home. Three short bursts enabled him to record in his logbook 'one He 111 probably destroyed. Rear gunner caught a packet'. They made three more patrols that night, and during the last, in the early hours of the 12th, caught a He 111 (probably 6N+HH of 7./KG 100). It crashed into the sea in flames north of Malta, adding Shipard to No 89 Sqn's growing list of aces. He bagged another the following night.

Also up on the night of 12 October was Flt Sgt Maurice Pring, and whilst patrolling over Castelvetrano airfield, on Sicily, he brought down a Z.1007bis as it approached to land, as well as a He 111 – he identified both victims as 'Heinkels'. Pring claimed a Ju 88 (his fourth kill) six nights later, and became an ace over Calcutta the following January.

The *blitz* continued, and on the night of the 14th Shipard and Oxby located a He 111 of II./KG 100 to the east at 12,500 ft. Lowering his undercarriage to reduce speed, Shipard closed in and opened fire. The Heinkel exploded, showering the sea with debris. It represented the pair's final victory over Malta. Three nights later, on the 17th, after another day of heavy raids, Flg Off Charles Crombie and Sgt R C Moss were over Catania. Soon after arriving, they spotted an aircraft below and attacked head-on. Uffz Hoffmann's I./KG 54 Ju 88 B3+UL hit the runway and exploded. It was the Australian's fifth confirmed success.

Also with the No 89 Sqn detachment was Sqn Ldr Derek Pain. On the night of 5 November he chased a Cant that had bombed St Paul's Bay and shot it down in flames off Gozo, elevating himself to ace status. Two nights later, during a patrol over Sicily, Pain is thought to have hit balloon cables and crashed to become a prisoner of war with Sgt Briggs. Over the same area Charles Crombie downed a Ju 88, but it might have been Pain's Beaufighter – illustrating an ever-present hazard of night intruding.

STRIKES FROM MALTA

Offensive strike operations from Malta took an increasing toll of Rommel's vital supplies, and this campaign intensified after the opening of the El Alamein offensive. But Malta's ordeal by bomb continued. In early November No 272 Sqn moved to Ta Kali for offensive operations, while No 252 Sqn remained in North Africa to harry the retreating enemy from El Alamein.

The advance in Egypt and the landings in French North Africa transformed the situation, lifting Malta's siege. No 272 Sqn was led by Sqn Ldr Anthony Watson, who damaged a He 115 on 11 November. It was forced down then destroyed on the water to become his fifth success.

The squadron's first major attack came the next day when Watson led six aircraft to Pantelleria. There they found six SM.79 transports and destroyed the lot, four going down in flames. Watson claimed two and shared a third to score his final victories. Posted to No 227 Sqn as CO shortly afterwards, Pain was subsequently wounded by flak attacking shipping on 22 January 1943. His replacement at No 272 Sqn was Wg Cdr J K Buchanan, who would become the greatest strike Beaufighter pilot of them all.

On 13 November it was No 227 Sqn's turn to engage the enemy when Wg Cdr Masterman led a section with Schmidt, now a flight lieutenant, but because of mist the formation became dispersed. As it cleared, Schmidt and South African pilot Lt Reg Clements spotted a Do 24 flying boat, which was promptly despatched into the sea. Turning away, Schmidt spotted a formation of 16 Ju 52/3ms in three elements. Attacking immediately, he damaged one with his first burst and then destroyed another. He continued to attack, and shot down a second as another formation of about 30 SM.82 transports appeared. Masterman's section pounced on them and shot one down. Clements also downed two in company with Sgt Franklin. Finally, the CO shared a second victory with Sgt Megone. Several Beaufighters, including Schmidt's, were hit by return fire, and he struggled home on one engine.

No 227 Sqn's attack on Bizerta the next day was less successful, and several Beaufighters were shot down, one by a Bf 109 flown by Uffz Hartmut Klotzer of III./JG 53. He was then set upon by American Plt Off Carl Johnson and shot down into the sea. Johnson quickly followed up this rare victory over such a dangerous adversary by shooting down a Ju 88. On the way home the CO and Lt Clements spotted a SM.75 transport which they shot down. It was Masterman's fifth success, four of them shared.

John Buchanan opened his account on the 20th when he shot down a He 115 floatplane off Linosa Island and then claimed a Cant Z.506 in the same area the next day. Carl Johnson of No 227 Sqn led a patrol, which met two Ju 52/3ms and the young pilot shot them down in less than a minute to

Australian Flg Off Ern Coate (right) flew with No 272 Sqn from Malta in late 1942. He destroyed ten aircraft in the air and one on the ground, and was awarded the DFC and Bar in early 1943 (*via B Cull*)

Four of Malta's successful strike Beaufighter pilots relax in Ta Kali's Mess on Boxing Day 1942. They are, from left to right, Wg Cdr Cedric Masterman, CO of No 227 Sqn (two and four shared victories), Wg Cdr John Buchanan, CO No 272 Sqn (ten and three shared victories), Sqn Ldr Anthony Watson, previously CO of No 272 Sqn, who has just returned from being shot down (six and two shared victories), and Flt Lt Peter Cobley of No 272 Sqn (at least two shared victories and six damaged) (*C A Masterman*)

become an ace. But the following day, while attacking a torpedo boat, he was hit by return fire and crashed into the sea. Both Johnson and his navigator, Sgt R A Webb, were killed. As the same time, Schmidt spotted a Ju 52/3m flying north. He made a beam attack, firing a couple of two-second bursts, and the transport broke up and crashed on fire to mark his fifth victory.

Another successful pilot was lost to flak in the early hours of 24 November when Lt Reg Clements failed to return, he and his navigator, Plt Off Ken Pollard, becoming PoWs. It has been reported that they told their captors about shooting down a Ju 52/3m near Trapani before they crashed. With at least four victories (two of them shared), he was the most successful South African Air Force Beaufighter pilot.

The strike pilots were also taking a toll, and on 27 November Buchanan's four-ship formation had a brief combat with two Bf 110s. Buchanan shot one down to 'make ace', and he quickly followed this up by bringing down a Ju 88. The next day he downed a SM.79, while two others shared a Sicilian-based SM.79 – the half-share made Flt Lt Ron Rankin an ace too.

Another Malta pilot who was to reach this distinction was No 227 Sqn's Plt Off R S 'Red' Modera. On 8 December he was flying with a section that encountered a formation of enemy transports, and he was credited with the destruction of one of the escorting Bf 110s for his first claim. A week later Dallas Schmidt led another sweep to the west. Passing Lampedusa on their way home, the Beaufighter crews ran into another formation of about 15 Ju 52/3ms. In the melee Schmidt poured fire into a transport, while Modera shot down one and probably destroyed another, with a third damaged. From the rear cockpit Sgt Hodges shot down yet another with his gun. On Christmas Day both Schmidt and his CO, Cedric Masterman completed their tours on Malta.

TO EL ALAMEIN AND AFTER

In North Africa, Rommel's offensive at the end of May 1942 marked the start of several months of heavy and confused fighting which ended on the Alamein line. Both Nos 252 and 272 Sqns attacked enemy transport aircraft at bases deep in the rear. It was dangerous work, as evidenced by a strafing mission on Derna at the end of June. After Flg Off Gunnis had

With 250-lb bombs under its wings, No 227 Sqn's Mk VIC JL519/P sets off on another anti-shipping sortie in early 1943. In April of that year, the aircraft was usually flown by Flg Off Raymond Modera, who, the following month, was to become the latest strike Beaufighter pilot to become an ace. But on 1 May, during a sortie from Gambut, JL519, flown by Flg Off Tommy Deck, was hit by flak and force-landed in Turkey. Deck was able to rejoin the squadron on 8 June after a brief internment (*HQ 201 Gp Records*)

Beaufighter IF X7677/TJ-Z of No 272 Sqn was unusual in being a night fighter variant assigned to a strike squadron, having been transferred in from No 89 Sqn. It was flown by a number of aces during July 1942, including Australian Flg Offs Ron Rankin and Ern Coate and Canadian Plt Off Albert Smith. The aircraft was lost over the Mediterranean on 20 August. The markings date this photograph as having been taken in July or August 1942 (*via M Hodgson*)

During mid 1942 a new nightfighter unit began forming, and No 46 Sqn's first victory was scored in June. On 21 August the CO, Wg Cdr G A Reid, shot down a Ju 88 of III./LG 1 in this aircraft, X7779 (*R W Richardson*)

destroyed two Ju 52/3ms he was hit and badly wounded in the legs. His navigator, Sgt Waller, applied tourniquets and managed to fly the aircraft home to be awarded a DFM. Anti-transport patrols were also flown.

The new No 46 Sqn had its first success when, on the early morning of 16 June, an intruder was brought down north of Alexandria. Plt Off Paul Sage claimed the second (a Ju 88) before the month was out, and then downed another on 4 July, as was recorded in a contemporary report;

'Contact was made near Aboukir, and I visually identified the aircraft as a Ju 88. I fired a short burst from 100 ft dead astern and slightly below at a height of 11,000 ft. The starboard engine and fuselage of the aircraft caught fire and it blew up in mid air at 0305 hrs. Crew taken prisoner.'

The squadron made further claims on that and subsequent nights. The month ended very successfully for the new boys of No 46 Sqn with three bombers shot down, including a He 111 falling to Kiwi Flt Lt R M 'Rusty' Mackenzie over Aboukir on 31 July. It was his second kill.

Fighting continued throughout August, and the month ended with the start of Rommel's final offensive on the 31st that began the Battle of Alam Halfa. As ever, the strike squadrons remained fully committed, and on 3 September two of No 252 Sqn's Beaufighters went for a He 111 on anti-submarine escort. Sgt George Tuckwell of No 272 Sqn (temporarily assigned to No 252) attacked first, putting an engine out of action and damaging the fuselage. Then Sgt Stan Kernaghan closed in and fired a long burst. The Heinkel hit the sea and broke up. It was the third of Tuckwell's five victories, but frustratingly his Canadian wingman ended his tour with four and a probable.

That night No 46 Sqn was also engaged over the rear areas. Plt Off

Michael Davison's sortie towards Alamein was described as follows;

'Four exhaust flames were seen to starboard from 1500 ft. Visual obtained, our aircraft then got behind and a two-second burst was given at a range of 100 yards. The starboard engine of the Ju 88 caught fire and bits hit our aircraft, which broke away to port to avoid collision. The enemy aircraft was then lost to sight, but a glow was seen on both sides of our machine. Last seen, the Ju 88 was burning brightly on the sea. No sign of survivors.'

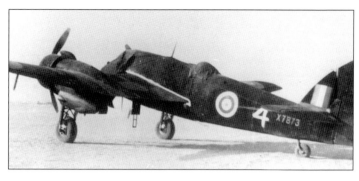

Another of No 46 Sqn's Beaufighters was X7873/4, which was sometimes flown during August 1942 by Kiwi Sqn Ldr R M Mackenzie, who scored three and one shared victories (*R W Richardson*)

Michael Davison went on to destroy another 11 enemy aircraft.

The decisive Battle of El Alamein began with a barrage on 23 October, and in an effort to reduce the enemy's ability to manoeuvre, it was vital to maintain the pressure on fuel supplies. Three days later Beaufighters from Gianaclis-based Nos 252 and 272 Sqns flew a coordinated attack on an Axis convoy. North-west of Sidi Barrani they also encountered five He 111s and attacked immediately. Plt Off Albert Smith of No 272 Sqn destroyed one for his fifth victory. Making a head-on attack, Sgt Kernaghan's Beaufighter was hit by around 40 bullets – an experience he described as 'like sitting in a car during a hailstorm'. He positioned himself above and behind the bombers, and seeing one flying slightly out of formation, he quickly dived and hit it so effectively that it exploded. Some of the debris damaged the starboard wing of his Beaufighter.

Soon afterwards came the breakthrough, followed by the Anglo-American Operation *Torch* landings in Algeria and Morocco, which brought more Beaufighter units into theatre.

ACTION OVER ALGERIA AND TUNISIA

With airfields secured, No 255 Sqn flew into Maison Blanche, near Algiers, on 15 November to become the first nightfighter unit in Algeria. But its Beaufighters' AI equipment had been removed in England as a security measure. Initially, therefore, they were of limited value against increasing enemy night attacks, one of which destroyed five of the squadron's Beaufighters on the 20th. No 600 Sqn had also arrived at Blida, a little to the south-west, while on the 26th No 89 Sqn's Beaufighters flew in to Algiers to provide a proper night defence. Now commanded by Wg Cdr J A 'Prof' Leathart, who had 6.5 victories from his time as CO of No 54 Sqn in 1940, it began patrols the following night.

On 27/28 November Australian Plt Off Arthur Spurgin and American Sgt Paul Park Norris gave No 89 Sqn a conspicuous start by downing two He 111s, while a fifth was destroyed by Flg Off John Etherton. Both Etherton and Spurgin would become aces within a few weeks. A few nights later No 600 Sqn claimed its first overseas victory, and in early December No 89 Sqn's detachment claimed three more Heinkels before moving to Bone.

Having replaced its losses, No 255 Sqn enjoyed its first success over Algiers in the early hours of 6 December when Flg Off Mike Gloster, with Plt Off J F Oswald, shot down a He 111 over Bone. He opened fire and

Although never quite an ace, Canadian Sgt Stan Kernaghan of No 252 Sqn was an aggressive pilot who gained four destroyed and a probable during his tour in the Mediterranean (*S J Kernaghan*)

sent it straight in, and soon afterwards a second fell to his guns. Almost immediately he closed on a third over Bone, and it blew up – these were the future ace's first victories. Flg Off Geoffrey Humes also claimed two He 111s that night, all five of No 255 Sqn's victims coming from KG 100.

The following night the flight commander, New Zealander Sqn Ldr John Player, with Flt Lt Lammer as navigator, were off Bone when they located a He 111 and shot it down. They then chased a Cant Z.1007, which fell in flames west of the port. Almost immediately they found another Cant, which blew up under Player's fire to complete his hat trick.

On 9 December No 255 Sqn sent a detachment forward to Bone to operate alongside No 89 Sqn's element, which was being kept busy. the latter unit's John Etherton shot down three II./KG 54 Ju 88s on the night of the 12th to become the theatre's first night ace.

Also flying from Bone (in X8010) was Flg Off Douglas Greaves, and he and Wt Off F M Robbins downed a He 111 in flames on 12/13 December – the first of their nine kills. They were to enjoy more success over the next few nights, although on the 14th the Ju 88 that they were attacking exploded and damaged their Beaufighter so badly that Robbins baled out and Greaves crash-landed at Bone. Two days later the detachment moved to Setif, from where, on the night of the 20th, Greaves chased a He 111 (possibly a Z.1007). He fired and hit it before his cannon jammed, but it had been mortally damaged. GCI controllers saw it come to earth, so Greaves was credited with his fourth kill.

Another new unit went into action on Christmas Eve when No 153 Sqn gained its first victory. Its CO, Wg Cdr Bill Moseby, told the author how it had happened;

'Having flown from the UK without AI radar fitted, we were useless at night, but we did fly some patrols in the daytime, and had some success on the third day when Plt Off Ken Rayment shot down a Ju 52 (actually

No 255 Sqn Beaufighter V8819 flies a day patrol over the rugged Algerian terrain in early 1943 when the unit was achieving considerable success against intruding German and Italian bombers (D H Greaves)

Well wrapped in dust-sheets at Reghaia in mid-1943, No 153 Sqn Beaufighter VIF EL177 awaits its next sortie. Around this time it was flown by future aces Sqn Ldr Laurie Styles (who was also a flight commander) and Flg Off Peter Williamson (via R C Sturtivant)

No 153 Sqn aircrew gather in front of Beaufighter VIF TB-A at Maison Blanche in July 1943 to mark the unit's 50th victory. Standing, from left to right, are Wg Cdr W G Moseby (two victories), Flg Off Peter Williamson (nine victories), Sgt Serbrooke, Flg Off Jack Haddon (four victories), Flt Sgt I W Grew (two victories), Sgt Cheetham, Flg Off N Barker, Flt Lt George Evans, Sqn Ldr George McLannahan, Sqn Ldr Laurie Styles (five victories), Flg Off Leslie Stephenson (ten victories) and Flg Off Ken Rayment (six victories). Kneeling, from left to right, are Sgt Thompson, Flg Off Bovey, Flg Off H West, Sgt J Ayliffe and Flg Off L Smith (*W G Moseby*)

a Fiat RS.14 – Editor) in the Italy-Tunis reinforcement area. When our AI radar arrived, along with the rest of the squadron, we settled down to the real job of intercepting enemy raiders at night who were attacking the Malta and Tobruk convoys. We operated between Oran and Bizerta.'

Another of No 255 Sqn's future aces, Plt Off Philip Kendall, also got into the action to achieve his first victory over Africa in the early hours of 8 January 1943. Patrolling over Bone, he was vectored onto a Cant Z.1007, which he promptly shot down. Further east, No 89 Sqn's detachment at Benina, near the Libyan port of Benghazi, was also in action that night. Flg Off Mervyn Shipard and Sgt Douggie Oxby brought down two Ju 88s and a He 111, while Flt Sgt Harry Shead bagged a second Heinkel (the third of his five victories). Shipard's I./LG 1 Ju 88 fell near Tobruk, its pilot, Ofw Isachsen, being a Knight's Cross holder. A week later, over Tobruk, Shipard and Oxby shot down two II./LG 1 Ju 88s. Mervyn Shipard vividly described the final victories, which made him the war's leading RAAF nightfighter pilot;

'I was scrambled and ordered to patrol between base and Gambut. After various vectors, I obtained a visual on the enemy aircraft dead ahead and slightly above. It was flying so slowly and jinking so much that exhausts were not visible until I was within 300 yards. I opened fire from dead astern at a range of 150 yards, closing to 100 yards with a three-second burst, and saw a large number of strikes on both engines and fuselage. The Ju 88 belched smoke and went down steeply to starboard.

'After the first combat, I was told to orbit, then given various vectors. The enemy aircraft appeared to be jinking approximately 30 degrees, and flying very slowly. My operator obtained contact with the Ju 88 at right angles, crossing from starboard to port – well above. A large number of corrections were given, and I obtained a visual on the aircraft's silhouette. No exhausts were seen at first as it was flying very slowly. I closed in at 140

The serial of this nightfighter Beaufighter VIF of No 89 Sqn is not clear, but is thought to be V8447/N. If so, then it is seen at Castel Benito, in Libya, on 3 August 1943 after a tyre had burst on landing, causing the aircraft to swing and crash. The pilot was 17-victory ace Wg Cdr Dennis David, who had assumed command of the unit two weeks earlier, and had mainly flown this aircraft (*via M Hodgson*)

Beaufighter IF V8219 of No 89 Sqn was a very successful aircraft, being flown in combat in mid-1942 by a number of aces. The first was Flg Off Nevil Reeves, who shot down a Ju 88 on 30 July, followed two weeks later by a Z.1007 for his fifth victory. On the night of 23 September, Flg Off Michael Kinmonth destroyed an Italian Ju 87 for his third success and, finally, on the night of 11 November, Flg Off Mervyn Shipard 'made ace' with this aircraft when he downed a He 111 and claimed a second as a probable (*via J D Oughton*)

One of the most successful Beaufighter teams in North Africa comprised No 153 Sqn's Flg Offs Leslie Stephenson (left) and G A Hall. In April and May 1943 they shot down six Ju 88s, including three on the night of 23 May (*via G R Pitchfork*)

mph and had to weave violently to avoid overshooting, as the Ju 88 appeared to be travelling at approximately 100 mph. I eventually came in from dead astern and opened fire at a range of 100 yards with a four-second burst. The aircraft immediately caught fire in both engines and fuselage and went down vertically in flames.'

Further west, on 18 January Douglas Greaves became the first of No 255 Sqn's pilots to become an ace over Africa when he shot another Cant Z.1007 down into the sea in flames.

With almost total Allied dominance of the daytime skies, many enemy bombing attacks were planned for the hours of darkness, and so the nightfighter units were kept busy. No 89 Sqn's CO, 'Prof' Leathart gained his only night victory during February, and at the end of the month Flg Off Michael Kinmonth became the unit's latest ace shortly before it moved to Castel Benito.

To replace it, No 108 Sqn was formed at Shandur, on the Suez Canal, to fly night patrols over Egypt, Malta and Libya. It was commanded by Wg Cdr 'Jasper' Read, and included some very notable pilots, including fellow New Zealander Flt Lt Victor Verity, who had 7.5 victories, and Flt Lt Henry Edwards with seven. Another pilot who joined the new squadron was Flt Lt Dickie Martin, who had become an ace while flying Hurricanes in the desert. He wrote of his brief time with the squadron specially for this book;

'I was only in No 108 Sqn of Beaufighter nightfighters from May to July 1943. At the time we had one flight based at Bersis, outside Benghazi, and the other flight in Malta. The CO was a lively chap called "Jasper" Read, who scored a number of victories, and another pilot was a chap called Verity, who went on to become an ace. It was Verity who, over Sicily on the night of 17 April 1943, claimed No 108 Sqn's first success when he inter-

cepted a He 111 over Trapani. He opened fire and hit the starboard engine, after which the bomber spun away and exploded.'

A Beaufighter from the unit's detachment in Malta, flown by Flg Off Bob Cowper, later patrolled the Sicilian airfield of Marsala three nights later. He intercepted an Me 410, which he damaged for his first combat claim. Later that night Flg Off Reg 'Fingers' Foster, with Plt Off 'Apple' Newton, intercepted Uffz Kohler's 10./ZG 26 Ju 88C at 10,000 ft over Marsala. He hit the fuselage and starboard engine, sending the aircraft crashing to its destruction. It was the second of Foster's nine confirmed successes.

Action continued from Algeria and Tunisia too, with day standby also being mounted. At approximately 1700 hrs on 13 April, nine No 255 Sqn Beaufighters were scrambled to intercept bombers attacking a convoy south of Sardinia. An hour later they sighted the enemy low over the sea, and Plt Off Kevin O'Sullivan attacked and damaged a He 111. It was his first claim, and may subsequently have been upgraded to start him on the road to acedom. The unit then split, and in the ensuing melee several other pilots claimed as the attack was broken up.

As well as attacking Allied shipping, the enemy made desperate efforts to re-supply its forces in Tunisia by air. There were regular encounters with enemy transport formations, and some pilots swiftly rose to prominence. One was Flt Sgt Alwyn Downing, who on 30 April became the only Beaufighter pilot to become an 'ace in a day'. One of his colleagues told the author;

'"Barry" Downing was about 19, and trying to grow a moustache. It was a miserable wispy affair. We had moved forward to Bone, and "Barry", or "Ace" as he was known, came back in the early light with his gun ports shot away. In answer to the question, "How many did you get?" he answered simply, "Five". And he had too! At first light he had been

having a look round off the coast of southern Sardinia when he came across a formation of Junkers 52s. He attacked one after the other with his almost inexhaustible supply of ammunition. They were apparently troop carriers because soldiers were firing back at him with small arms from the windows. He was awarded an immediate DFM.'

Five days later, during an evening patrol, Flg Off Philip Kendall of No 255 Sqn intercepted another group of Ju 52/3ms off Cap Serat, shooting one down to give him his all important fifth victory.

The final acts of the campaign in North Africa were now being played out. Axis forces in Tunisia surrendered on 13 May, but enemy aircraft were still attacking shipping and the African ports. No 219 Sqn became operational at Bone in late June, and it was soon in action. The unit's CO was experienced night ace Wg Cdr Archie Boyd, who shot down two Ju 88s on the 30th to score the unit's first African success. On 9 July the USAAF's 414th Night Fighter Squadron (NFS), flying Beaufighters, became operational. It was duly followed by three more.

THE ITALIAN CAMPAIGN

The invasion of Sicily, codenamed Operation *Husky*, began on 10 July 1943. It opened up another area of operations, and among other units, No 108 Sqn patrolled over the beaches. The following day, near Syracuse, Flg Off Bob Cowper scored his first confirmed victory. But as the Ju 88 exploded, debris from it damaged the Beaufighter, forcing the crew to bale out. On the 13th, to the east of Syracuse, 'Jasper' Read became an ace when he shot down a He 111 and a Ju 88. Then came an incredible run of success which saw him down five more bombers in just a week.

A few nights later Capt N H Lindsay of the 415th NFS claimed the first victory for a USAAF Beaufighter when he sent a He 115 crashing into the sea. Most Beaufighter units were involved in *Husky,* and some were soon operating from captured airstrips which often came under attack. On the night of 11 August, Sqn Ldr Desmond Hughes of No 600 Sqn was vectored to the Catania area, where the airfield was under attack. He was later to recall;

'I was on patrol at the right time, and with very accurate GCI control, I was put in AI contact with four Ju 88s, which obligingly flew in nicely spaced intervals. Three of these masterly directions from my navigator,

Four USAAF nightfighter squadrons flew the Beaufighter in the Mediterranean theatre, and although they produced no aces, they did claim a respectable number of victories. The first came on 15 July 1943 when Capt N H Lindsay of the 415th NFS shot a He 115 down into the sea off Catania (*H Levy*)

On the night of 16 August 1943 Sqn Ldr 'Black' Morton shot down a He 111 over the Mediterranean. Flying V8868 with Flg Off Bailey, it was his final victory, taking his total to six and four shared destroyed – all but two of them achieved during the Battle of Britain with No 603 Sqn on Spitfire Is. The tropical climate, however, took its toll, and the following month Morton was repatriated due to poor health (*David Ross Collection*)

Flying V8881/FK-L near Bizerta on the night of 6 September 1943, No 219 Sqn's CO Wg Cdr Archie Boyd shot down a He 111 to claim his penultimate victory – his 10th, and last, kill came 12 days later. Boyd had achieved all of his successes at the controls of a Beaufighter over a two-and-a-half-year period (*H Levy*)

Flg Off Laurie Dixon, brought visual contact, and one bomber after another fell to the devastating punch of the Beaufighter's four cannon and six machine guns. The fourth Ju 88 we followed into the AA fire zone, and as we closed in I found we were collecting all the unpleasantness intended for the enemy bombers.'

Credited with three destroyed, they had their final success with No 600 Sqn a few days later when they got a Ju 87 off Syracuse at dawn. Hughes flew his final sortie with the unit at the end of September, by which time the nightfighters had claimed 34 aircraft shot down in August. Between 8-18 September, 19 more were claimed by Nos 219, 255 and 600 Sqns.

In North Africa, No 219 Sqn was also kept busy. On the night of 6 September, a large raid attacked Bizerta, and eight Beaufighters were scrambled, shooting down four of the Heinkels. Three of them fell to Sqn Ldr W R L Beaumont in just 20 minutes, as he later described;

'Scrambled from La Sebala at 2025 hrs, we were told to go north from base at 7000 ft. Control gave a vector of 320 degrees, and told me to increase speed as there were 30+ enemy aircraft about. A contact was obtained to the west against the last light. We went all out and passed three other enemy aircraft crossing starboard to port, declining to divert onto them as we had chosen a target. We retained contact as the target did fantastic weaves port and starboard, climbing and diving down. The range closed to 600 ft and I opened fire just as the enemy aircraft made a turn to starboard, giving me a slight deflection shot. It flew into the cone of fire and exploded in the sky, diving down in flames into the sea and burning on the surface.

'We then turned south on 190 degrees and soon got another contact straight ahead at 8000 ft at three miles range, slightly above and crossing to port. The target was above, climbing into the moon. Range reduced to 2000 ft and we held there, but visual was not obtained due to dazzle from the moon. We jockeyed for position and closed to the starboard side of the enemy aircraft at 600 ft. I gave a two-second burst and it exploded in the air, turning over and going down in flames on the coast.'

He went on to bring down another He 111, while the fourth fell to the guns of his CO, Wg Cdr Boyd, who scored his penultimate victory.

Offensive fighter patrols were mounted to the north-east of Corsica to prevent enemy transport aircraft conducting re-supply and evacuation operations. One of the units involved was No 39 Sqn, which was a strike

unit which had recently swapped its Beaufort IIs for Beaufighter Xs. The first patrols were flown on 23 September, when five transports were shot down. The next day eight more were destroyed. Overall, No 39 Sqn claimed 11 Ju 52/3ms and four SM.82s shot down for the loss of three Beaufighters. Two fell on each day to Flg Off Neil Cox, who eventually gained his fifth victory flying Tempests just before the end of the war. Flt Lt Derek White, who earlier in the year had claimed four victories flying Beaufighters with the Coastal Reconnaissance Flight, also shot down an SM.82 on the 24th to become an ace.

By now there was a general reduction in enemy air activity over Italy during the day, although there were still regular encounters by night, and over the Aegean, where a bitter war against enemy coastal shipping was being waged. There were also occasional encounters over the Mediterranean, where, in early 1944, 2Lt Rayford Jeffery (with his navigator Lt Bill Henderson) of the 417th NFS made the squadron's first claim. He recalled;

'I received a call from ground control that they had a bogey, and they gave me the vector to intercept back towards Majorca. It didn't take long for Henderson to lock-on and start giving me headings for an intercept. It was just beginning to get light, and I got a visual at about a quarter-of-a-mile, crossing right to left at an altitude of about 50 ft. I identified the aircraft as a Ju 88. I was at 3000 ft and started my attack from the rear and above, rapidly closing the range to 300 ft. In the darkness, I saw flashes from the tracer ammunition of the enemy as his turret gun opened fire on me. Aiming just forward of the nose of the bogey, I fired a very short burst and saw hits on his cockpit and down across the wing,

Beaufighter X LX907/W of No 39 Sqn was the regular aircraft of Plt Off M C Hyslop, who flew it on its first operation on 8 August 1943 when the unit attacked shipping off Naples. On 23 September, with Hyslop again at the controls, it was part of a formation led by Flg Off Derek White in LX788/I which attacked three German-marked SM.82 transports participating in the evacuation of Corsica. All were shot down in flames, White's victory being his fifth. The following day, Hyslop was again flying this aircraft in a formation led by squadron CO, Wg Cdr N B Harvey, which attacked three Ju 52/3ms south-east of Bastia. Again, all the transports were shot down
(*via R C B Ashworth*)

The most successful pilot in No 39 Sqn's slaughter of the transports off Corsica in September 1943 was Flg Off Neil Cox, who shot down four. He became an ace just before the end of the war when he shared in the destruction of a Me 262 over Germany (*via C F Shores*)

inboard of the left engine. His left wing separated from the fuselage and it rolled over and dived into the water. I circled above looking for survivors, but did not see any.

'En route back to base, the routine hum of my engines decreased by half and the "Beau" tried to roll on me. I'll be damned if the enemy gunner's fire hadn't taken out one of my engines, and these birds didn't like to fly on just one! I did manage to make it back for a safe wheels-down landing – no mean feat on one engine. This had been my first kill, and also the first one for our squadron.'

At the end of March he shot down another and was again hit, but this time made a wheels-up landing.

On 4 June 1944 the Allies entered Rome, and after the landings in France most German night bombers left Italy. NSGr 9's Ju 87s remained, however, and they suffered heavy losses – 13 to Nos 255 and 600 Sqns in July and nine more in August. By this time the Allies had virtual air supremacy over Italy by day and night. Over the Ancona area on the night of 6 July, three Ju 87s were destroyed by Flg Off Bruce Bretherton of No 255 Sqn to make him an ace. In a contemporary account he wrote;

'The bandit tried to escape north but without success, and at a range of 500 ft I opened fire on an aircraft identified as a Ju 87. It burst into flames and crashed north-west of Ancona. The patrol was resumed and an aircraft identified as another Ju 87 was destroyed and crashed into a hill just outside Ancona. The patrol was again resumed offshore of Ancona, and after further vectors, contact and visual was gained on another Ju 87. Three short bursts given at a range of 300 ft saw the Stuka go down almost vertically with smoke pouring from it. It hit the ground west of Ancona.'

The following night Flt Lt Tim Reynolds got two more. He described the difficulty of intercepting these night raiders;

'Our first three kills were all Ju 87s, two in one night. They could practically hover compared with a "Beau", and if it had not been for the excellent forward visibility from the pilot's seat we should have lost them time and time again. The "Beau" in this respect was magnificent. Likewise, its slow-flying capabilities were reasonable enough, although the sight of us wallowing along behind a Ju 87 with full flap, undercart down, fully fine pitch and still overshooting the target had to be seen to be believed. It was not the world's most stable gun platform at this speed.'

His final kill (Ju 88A-4 F6+NP of 6(G)./122) came off the coast of Rimini at dawn on 1 August, making Reynolds an ace.

Seen visiting Foggia, in southern Italy, in late 1943, thimble-nosed Beaufighter VIF MM924/YD-L of No 255 Sqn was one of the aircraft which provided much of the night defence of the 8th Army over the next 18 months (*via J D Oughton*)

This superb shot of No 46 Sqn's Mk VIF V8708/S was taken at about the time the unit sent a detachment of aircraft to Gambut in September 1944. It has had its undersides painted black in direct contravention to standard RAF camouflage instructions then in place (*B J Wild*)

In addition to small coasters, the enemy used transport aircraft flying at night to supply its garrisons on numerous islands in the Aegean. In late September 1944 No 46 Sqn mounted a detachment at Gambut to work over the Aegean under the control of the GCI ship HMS *Ulster Queen*, of which the squadron recording officer wrote;

'Any misgivings which might have been had about the success of operations from this detachment have been entirely dispelled by the excellent and marvellous results obtained. Our score of enemy aircraft up to the end of the month is – 11 destroyed (two Do 24s, one Ju 188 and eight Ju 52s), one probable and three damaged. Heartiest congratulations to Wt Off Butler, our top scorer. He destroyed three on the first night.'

These actions made Roy Butler and his navigator, Wt Off R F Graham, the last Beaufighter team to attain ace status during the war, as well as one of the quickest. Of his first night's action, Butler wrote;

'I sighted two green lights crossing in front, port to starboard. I executed a hard starboard turn and closed in to approximately 250 yards and recognised a Do 24 flying at 300 ft. We attacked from dead astern and gave three short bursts. Our third caused a burst of flame from the wing. We pulled away to port and watched the enemy aircraft glide down in flames and crash into the sea, burning for five minutes. We returned to control, being vectored to another bogey crossing port to starboard. We obtained contact, decreased to 100 ft, closed in and obtained visual on a Ju 52 landplane. I gave one long burst at 200 yards dead astern and the enemy aircraft exploded violently and fell into the sea, burning for ten minutes with a huge pall of black smoke.

'I was informed that two further enemy aircraft were north, and at 2325 hrs contact was obtained. I closed but overshot, and the target disappeared. I returned to control and was directed to another target, and contact was obtained at 2.5 miles. I closed to 100 ft, overshot and recognised a Ju 52 floatplane. I executed a hard starboard orbit and regained contact at a range of four miles, closing on the enemy aircraft three miles off the coast of Trypete. I gave one short burst from 250 yards dead astern and observed strikes on the starboard engine, which caught fire. We followed up with a long burst and broke away hard to port, climbing. The enemy aircraft glided slowly down, struck the sea and burst into flames.'

Two nights later Butler and Graham, once more in ND243/Q, which was named *Kampala Queen* as No 46 Sqn was the Uganda unit, were again successful when they shot down a Ju 188 off the coast of Melos. On the first night of October the pair were again working with

In September 1944 No 46 Sqn sent a detachment to Gambut to co-operate with the Royal Navy in an effort to catch enemy transport aircraft attempting to re-supply German outposts in the Aegean at night. This scoreboard, adorning a battered propeller blade, shows how successful the detachment was! Flanking it is the leading crew with five aircraft destroyed, pilot Wt Off Roy Butler (right) and navigator Wt Off R F Graham (*F Baldwin*)

Ulster Queen, although this time flying KW160/A. Butler's report described the action;

'Vectored onto another target coming north at low level. We reduced to 500 ft turned and closed to ten miles west of Melos, recognising a He 111 heading 330 degrees at 250 ft. We opened fire from 200 yards and gave a three-second burst from dead astern. Strikes were observed and pieces flew off the tailplane. A fire started in the starboard wing root and smoke poured from the starboard engine. The aircraft broke away to port and was observed gliding down and striking the sea with a small momentary burst of flame. It then disappeared.'

This fifth victory, scored in as many days, took Butler to ace status.

Some of the No 46 Sqn Gambut detachment pose in front of Wt Off Butler's aircraft, KW160/A *Kampala Queen*, which was decorated with five swastikas. They are, standing from left to right, Wt Off Graham, Flt Sgt Freddie Baldwin, Wt Off Terry Phelan (two victories), Wt Off Dennis Hammond (three victories) and Flt Sgt Harrison. In the front row, from left to right, are Wt Offs Baptiste and Jim Bays (2.5 victories) (*F Baldwin*)

IN TROPICAL SKIES

In spite of devastating Japanese attacks on Ceylon and on Royal Navy vessels in the Bay of Bengal, there were still no radar-equipped nightfighters in India by the end of 1942. Night defence was an *ad hoc* arrangement, and in December the enemy mounted small-scale raids on the sprawling port of Calcutta, whose vital facilities made it the only strategic target within range of the enemy. A detachment of Beaufighters from No 89 Sqn was rushed out to India from Egypt, as recalled by Wg Cdr Tony O'Neill specially for this book;

'I was CO of No 293 Wing at the time. We had two Hurricane squadrons, Nos 146 and 17, for the air defence of Calcutta before the Beaufighters came out from the Middle East. The Japs sent over three Mitsubishi Ki-21 'Sally' long-range bombers on 23 December and the next night. On 14 January 1943, the squadron began building up at Dum Dum, Calcutta, when the nucleus of five AI Mk VIII radar-equipped Beaufighters and crews from No 89 Sqn arrived. No 176 Sqn was duly formed, and I was given command. Some of the pilots had several victories already. The squadron was responsible for the night defence of Calcutta from Japanese air attack, and was immediately operational.'

The new arrivals were soon in action, for on the night of 15 January a formation of Japanese Army Air Force (JAAF) Ki-21s of the 98th *Sentai* headed towards the city in bright moonlight. A contemporary account described them as 'completely uncamouflaged, and they gleamed like silver fishes as they flew over in formation'.

Among the Beaufighters airborne was X7776/M, flown by Sgt Maurice Pring, who was already credited with four victories and two damaged from his time in the Western Desert. He took off at 2145 hrs with his navigator, Wt Off C T Phillips, and was the first to sight the enemy. After clearing his tail, Pring closed on the unsuspecting enemy from the rear and promptly shot down three in very quick succession without encountering any return fire. The whole engagement lasted less than five

With its undersides painted black, and still to be fitted with its radar, one of No 176 Sqn's first Beaufighters is pictured soon after its arrival at Dum Dum in January 1943. These few aircraft made an immediate impact, halting bombing raids on Calcutta for almost a year (*G J Thomas*)

minutes, and Pring's success certainly put the new squadron on the map. More importantly, it gave a massive boost to civilian morale in Calcutta. These victories made Pring an ace, and he received an immediate DFM, with Phillips receiving a DFC.

The enemy returned a few nights later on the evening of the 19th. Airborne was Flg Off Charles Crombie, a nine-victory ace who (in X8164/G) duly added to his tally with the destruction of two 'Sallys' and a third as a probable over Budge Budge, to the south of Calcutta. During the initial attack the Beaufighter was hit and set ablaze by return fire, but in an act of cool courage, the crew remained in the aircraft and continued their attacks before the fuel tanks exploded and they had to bale out. Crombie was awarded a well-deserved DSO for his courage.

These heavy losses had an immediate effect, for Japanese night attacks on Calcutta stopped until the end of the year.

The following month the squadron moved to Baigachi, just east of the city, where its strength was gradually built up to eight Beaufighters and a flight of AI-equipped Hurricanes. Patrols were maintained over the city without incident.

The Beaufighter was also in service with other units in the area in the long-range strike role, although they saw little air combat. One exception was No 211 Sqn, which was formed at Phaphamau, in central India, during August. In October Wg Cdr Pat Meagher arrived as CO, with four victories to his name. The following month the squadron began operational training using under-wing rocket projectiles to work-up as a long range strike fighter unit.

By now No 176 Sqn was maintaining detachments to cover other vulnerable areas, one of which was at Ratmalana, in Ceylon, defending Colombo. It was here on 11 October 1943 that the squadron's next action came, as was recorded at the time;

'Flt Sgts L Atkinson and W Simpson increased the bag of the squadron tonight when they shot down a Japanese flying boat off Ceylon. The chase was a long one, commencing at 15,000 ft and ending at 6000 ft. Three fleeting contacts were made but lost, and after the Jap had gone out of GCI range, Flt Sgt Atkinson obtained a visual at 6000 yards range, closed in and shot away the starboard engine. Another burst was sufficient to set the Jap on fire and send him spiralling into the sea, exploding as he went. What a wizard sight!'

Their victim was an Imperial Japanese Navy (IJN) Kawanishi H6K 'Mavis' from the Andaman Islands.

With such a large and potentially vulnerable 'patch', it was decided to move a second dedicated night-fighter squadron to the area. Egypt-based No 89 Sqn was selected, and a few days after No 176 Sqn's latest success the unit began its move to Ceylon. By 25 October it was established at Vavuniya. The unit was led by Wg Cdr Denis David, previously a Hurricane pilot with 17 victories. He recalled in his autobiography;

Flt Sgt Maurice Pring enjoyed early success over Calcutta when he destroying three Ki-21s on the night of 15 January 1943 – just 24 hours after the Beaufighter detachment had arrived from the Middle East to form No 176 Sqn. He also became an ace in the process, and was awarded an immediate DFM (*J A O'Neill*)

On 19 January 1943 Flg Off Charles Crombie (right), who had already scored nine victories, attacked a Japanese bomber force over Calcutta. In spite of his aircraft being set on fire, he proceeded to shoot down two of them, before successfully baling out – a feat which earned him the DSO. He is seen here with his CO, Wg Cdr Tony O'Neill, who also had several victories to his name (*J A O'Neill*)

'After the desert, Ceylon appeared to the squadron as a veritable Garden of Eden. The day after our arrival, we made our aircraft operational for nightfighting and started affiliation with Ceylon's ground control. To my great relief it was of a high standard. I sent a detachment to Ratmalana and one to Madras. We still had only the few technicians who had flown out with us.'

The unit picked up where it had left off in the Middle East when, on 11 November, Flt Lt J G Astbury and Flg Off Ashworth of the Ratmalana detachment downed a 'Mavis'. Wg Cdr David described his feelings;

'Imagine our delight when, the day after they had set up for business, the detachment at Ratmalana destroyed a large Japanese Navy flying boat – a Kawanishi H6K – which had been going to bomb Colombo. The Japanese did not expect nightfighters of the calibre of the Beaufighter to be in the area. The esteem in which the locals held our squadron was enhanced. We were flavour of the month!'

The Japanese did not attempt to bomb Colombo at night again. The Madras detachment also found some action when another flying boat was attacked, as the record book reported;

'After receiving vectors, our aircraft obtained contact, resulting in visual acquisition. An attack was made from astern with slight deflections, and cannon strikes were seen on the port inboard motor. Machine gun strikes were also observed on the port wing tip. When last seen, the enemy aircraft was diving to starboard. Our aircraft followed, but was unable to keep contact of the contact. Claim result – one Japanese "Emily" four-engined flying boat damaged.'

Although a Kawanishi H8K 'Emily' was claimed, it is thought that the aircraft involved was actually another 'Mavis'.

STRUGGLE AT IMPHAL

After a reconnaissance build-up, the enemy finally returned to Calcutta on 5 December, but this time in daylight. Two of No 176 Sqn's Beaufighters were scrambled after an intruding Ki-46 'Dinah', which was detected by radar at 0615 hrs, but they were recalled as it flew out of range. Three hours later a large raid developed, and fighters, including No 176 Sqn's Hurricanes, were scrambled. On their second scramble they were bounced by escorting Zeros and four went down, with two pilots killed, including Maurice Pring. This was a particularly tragic loss, as the ace was about to be rested.

Two of No 176 Sqn's Beaufighter VIFs are prepared for the night's standby at Baigachi in early 1943. On the right is X7682/A, which was sometimes flown in early 1943 by Flt Sgt Maurice Pring (*P G Hill*)

After the loss of most of its Hurricane flight, the squadron was brought up to full strength with Beaufighters. But little was seen of the enemy. Soon afterwards, a flight was detached to Imphal to fly offensive sorties beyond the Chindwin into Burma, the first being to Heho and Meiktila on 6 February 1944. Nothing significant was found. Others flew patrols as far as the Andaman Islands. In the meantime, No 211 Sqn had moved east to Silchar from where it began operations over Burma in January.

There were still fleeting sightings of IJN flying boats, however, and the Beaufighters of No 89 Sqn's Madras detachment continued to be scrambled regularly throughout February without actual contact being made with the enemy. Japanese offensives in the Arakan and, more critically, at Imphal, in Assam, led to an upsurge in the fighting. No 211 Sqn, like the other strike units, continued long-range attacks, and on 15 February 1944 unit CO Wg Cdr Pat Meagher led a three-ship formation to the north of Akyab. Flying Beaufighter X LZ157/M with his navigator, Flg Off Woodhall, over Okshitpyin, they were attacked by Ki-43s. The squadron diary describes the encounter;

'The CO was intercepted by four "Oscars". He retaliated with a salvo of rockets, which missed, so he destroyed two of the bandits with his cannon. Altogether, the unit encountered many "Oscars" that day.'

Air combat was a rarity for the squadron, but the engagement made Meagher an ace. He was credited with one destroyed plus a probable – his previous claims were made in Spitfires and Hurricanes in 1941.

The greatest threats remained anti-aircraft fire and the weather, however. Among the most successful operations were those against airfields in the Rangoon area. On 6 March, for example, No 211 Sqn claimed two destroyed, two probables and six damaged on the ground. Two weeks later, on the 14th, Meagher added to his growing tally, as a contemporary account states;

'The attack on Meiktila and Annisaken was less successful, although the CO destroyed an Army 01 on the ground, and a bomber which he chased flew into a hill.'

The nightfighter units also helped in the struggle at Imphal, despite severe Japanese pressure, and No 176 Sqn moved a detachment there in

Beaufighter VIF V8741, which had previously served with No 68 Sqn in the UK, provides a backdrop for some of No 176 Sqn's hardworking groundcrew at Baigachi in early 1944. Unusually, the aircraft features a personal marking on its nose (K R Aunger)

March. On the night of the 16th one of its aircraft found the enemy, as a contemporary operational account records;

'At 0419 hrs Sgts Gosling and Grant were scrambled in the only available Beaufighter "N" (X8012 – Author). Climbing to 16,500 ft on a vector of 140 degrees, contact was made at 13,000 ft. The target at that moment apparently dropped its bomb load and made a diving turn to port. The resulting chase lasted about 20 minutes before a visual was obtained at 3000 ft level and 15 degrees to port. Closing in to 700 ft, the bandit was identified as an Army 97 (Ki-21). Dropping back to 300 yards, the pilot gave a burst with machine guns, followed by machine guns and cannons, resulting in a flash on the starboard wing inboard of nacelle, followed by orange flame. The target rapidly lost height, but the fire died down, leaving a large glow in the engine. Another four bursts were delivered with no observed results. The target hit the ground at Minthame. This was the squadron's first kill for some time.'

A detachment was also posted to Chittagong, where aircraft flew each night to the small strip at 'Reindeer', close to the frontline. The log for 3 April recalled;

'After a quiet day, the detachment had a couple of successful intercepts when Plt Off McCracken, with Flg Off R D Reikie, and Sgt Wallis, with Sgt Johnstone, were scrambled after a group of Japanese raiders. And after a very short chase Plt Off McCracken saw and identified a Type 99 "Lily" (Ki-48) twin-engined bomber, giving it 60 rounds of cannon. It exploded and went down. Meanwhile, Sgt Wallis, after an unsuccessful chase south after a second group of raiders, was turned back in time to intercept another "Lily", which he shot down with only 15 rounds per cannon.'

Rain, however, rendered 'Reindeer' unserviceable the following day.

JUNGLE ACE

No 211 Sqn continued its wide-ranging sorties too, and on 8 April Sqn Ldr Muller-Rowland encountered a rare Siamese Curtiss Hawk III biplane fighter over Thailand, as he reported;

'I saw a biplane at "nine o'clock", 1000 ft above me. I was at zero feet. The biplane was circling a petrol fire at Lambhun. I climbed, closing very fast from "five o'clock", and once beneath it, fired a two-second burst at 150 yards. The elevators of the aircraft fell off, and I was now above the

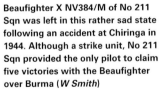

Beaufighter X NV384/M of No 211 Sqn was left in this rather sad state following an accident at Chiringa in 1944. Although a strike unit, No 211 Sqn provided the only pilot to claim five victories with the Beaufighter over Burma (*W Smith*)

enemy aircraft. As it fell away to starboard, I saw that it was a single-seater, and that the open cockpit was empty. I then saw a parachute fully open at about 500 ft. My observer saw the biplane crash and burst into flames.'

Nothing was seen of the JAAF until the 28 April, when Pat Meagher led an early morning sweep. His aircraft was enveloped in a thick haze, causing him to lose sight of his wingman;

'I was flying Beaufighter LZ157, one of a section of two detailed to attack rail communications. I took off at 0640 hrs and proceeded to Sagaing, where I lost my number two owing to fairly thick haze. I then proceeded south. I emerged from thick haze into thin and turned east to get my bearings. Almost immediately I found seven enemy fighters circling 3000 ft overhead. I was at deck level. I was going in the opposite direction to base, and was in such a generally disadvantageous position that the only hope appeared to be to fight it out. I turned 180 degrees and was attacked by two aircraft, one from port beam to quarter, the other from starboard beam to quarter. The attack was well co-ordinated.

'When both aircraft appeared to be in range, I throttled back completely. This seemed to upset the attack. The starboard aircraft overshot me and climbed right. I opened up and followed him, getting in about a half-second burst from dead astern at an angle of about 45 degrees to the horizontal. The enemy aircraft was hit and went up in flames. Almost at the same time there was a loud bang and I stalled. This was probably caused by my escape hatch, which came open. As I stalled, the aircraft spun to the right and I pulled out a few feet from the ground. This manoeuvre must have disconcerted the next pair to attack, as two enemy aircraft were observed falling in flames, closely interlocked.

'I next turned for base, as after the incipient spin I was again heading eastwards. A few seconds later I was attacked by another enemy aircraft from dead ahead, and also from ground level. This combat developed into a straight shooting match. Neither aircraft, because of the height, was able to depress the nose. Thus, the shells were going too high until the range became unpleasantly close. The enemy aircraft was firing what appeared to be 0.5-in tracer from two positions on either side of the airscrew. Just when I thought a collision was certain, I obtained a strike on the enemy aircraft's port wing root. The enemy aircraft slewed violently to his left

Beaufighter VIF ND220 was transferred to No 176 Sqn after serving in the UK. It was sometimes flown in early 1945 by Sqn Ldr John Etherton, who was one of the very few aces to fly the type in Burma (*R Lythgoe*)

Sqn Ldr John Etherton joined No 176 Sqn in December 1944, having previously claimed six victories during his time with No 89 Sqn in the Western Desert. He had no opportunity to increase his score in Burma, however (*via C G Jefford*)

and climbed. Nothing more was seen of the enemy, and a course was set for base. The enemy aircraft were believed to have been "Oscars".'

Meagher ended his report by claiming, 'One Oscar destroyed. One Oscar damaged. Two Oscar *Hari Kiri*!' Meager was the most successful Beaufighter pilot in Burma, and his victories were the last scored by a Beaufighter ace in the Far East.

In late August 1944 No 176 Sqn moved to Minneriya, in Ceylon, although by that stage there was little air threat to the island. It also maintained forward detachments at Chittagong and St Thomas Mount, near Madras, for night defence and intruder work. No 89 Sqn moved its HQ to Baigachi, although it too maintained widespread detachments.

On 7 December No 176 Sqn received a notable addition when six-kill ace Sqn Ldr John Etherton arrived with his navigator, Flt Lt Peasley. He flew his first trip on the 11th, but with the general lack of enemy activity saw no action before leaving the following April. On Christmas Day, No 89 Sqn's celebrations were interrupted by the destruction of three Ki-48s – two fell to Sqn Ldr R B Morison of the Chittagong detachment. The local Bengali newspapers waxed enthusiastic, and in an interview Morison was quoted as saying;

'It was a straightforward job. Wt Off Powell saw them and pointed them out to me, and one short burst in each case was enough. Both scraps were over in a matter of seconds. The enemy were above us and never had a chance. In fact, I doubt if the Japanese saw our aircraft because there was no return fire. I closed to point-blank range each time. The bombers burst into flames and, blazing fiercely, went straight down into the sea. One seemed to explode. It was a first-rate Christmas present. These were my first kills against the Japs.'

Not to be outdone, No 176 Sqn's detachment at Chittagong was also successful when Wt Off Vivian and Flt Sgt Lister scrambled in MM916/J. After direction from GCI, Lister brought his pilot in on AI. They had a long chase, but eventually hit another 'Lily'. Although initially claimed as damaged, three days later intelligence confirmed that the aircraft had indeed crashed near Magwe.

For the nightfighter units, there was to be little further action, but they were tasked with an increasing number of night 'Rhubarbs'. Defensive standbys were also maintained at forward strips, and during two sorties in the early hours of 4 March 1945 No 89 Sqn made its final claims of the war. Wt Offs H J C Johnson and M A Chalmers, in Mk VIF X8745, destroyed two bombers, the first over Mandalay and a second 15 miles to the south-east near Sadaung. A contemporary report described the action;

'This was a night of notable achievement on the part of the squadron, for in the course of it Wt Off H J C Johnson and navigator Wt Off M A Chalmers shot down two enemy aircraft – both "Lilys". They first scrambled at 0030 hrs and contact was made at a range of 7000 ft. A visual was obtained within 1000 ft, and Wt Off H J C Johnson followed the "Lily" down visually at a range of 700 ft after an initial burst of fire. When the Beaufighter finally had to break away owing to the proximity of the mountains, the "Lily" was in a vertical bank, with its port nacelle on fire.

'On returning to base, the groundcrew did well to refuel and re-arm the aircraft in the short space of 35 minutes. At 0155 hrs Wt Off Johnson again scrambled, and contact was made with a bogey north of the base.

The range was closed to 3000 ft and the bogey appeared well below. The Beaufighter reduced speed and height, and contact was maintained at 4000 ft. A visual was obtained at 1000 ft on the target, identified as a "Lily", which was weaving. Wt Off Johnson opened fire at 75 yards and there was return fire from the aircraft's ventral gun. The latter, however, caught fire, along the whole length of the belly. It slowed and nosed down suddenly, and Wt Off Chalmers saw a reflection of fire on the ground 15 miles south-east of Mandalay.'

Johnson's second claim was in fact a Ki-21 'Sally'. No 176 Sqn was to score one further victory, but with Japanese air strength largely beaten, and the change to Mosquitos imminent, the Beaufighter's time in the nightfighter role in Burma was over.

NEW GUINEA AND THE EAST INDIES

While RAF Beaufighters were engaged over India and Burma, they were also used by the RAAF against the Japanese over New Guinea and the sprawling islands of the Netherlands East Indies. Initially, 54 Beaufighter ICs had been ordered, and the first was delivered in March 1942 as No 30 Sqn RAAF was forming at Richmond, in New South Wales. Wg Cdr Brian 'Blackjack' Walker soon assumed command, leading the squadron in its deployment to Port Moresby, New Guinea, where it participated in the latter stages of the Battle of Milne Bay.

Mainly performing ground attack sorties, the Beaufighters had their first air-to-air engagement on 23 September 1942 when a strike was intercepted by six Zeros. These concentrated on A19-50, which managed to escape by diving to very low level and outpacing them. This was soon to become a standard tactic. The tempo of operations continued, with

Beaufighter VIF X7898/G of No 89 Sqn's detachment is seen at Sadaung, near Mandalay, in early 1945. It flew its first operation – a night 'Rhubarb' – on 10/11 January, with Wt Off H J C Johnson at the controls. On the night of 3 March he shot down two Ki-48 'Lilys' (in V8745) to claim the squadron's final victories of the war (*P H T Green Collection*)

No 30 Sqn being in the thick of the action, mainly undertaking low-level attacks. Typical was that of 17 November, when strafing runs on Lae airfield destroyed two 'Sallys' and four Zeros.

A few days later, on the 22nd, the squadron claimed its first aerial victory when, during another attack on Lae, a Zero that was spotted taking off was promptly shot down. That afternoon, Flt Lt Little, in A19-8 also attacked a Zero. He saw hits on the engine, which began smoking before the fighter disappeared. No 30 Sqn remained largely occupied undertaking ground attacks and anti-shipping strikes. It also played an important role in the capture of Buna, and during the Battle of the Bismarck Sea in March 1943 it helped destroy a convoy. In July of that year, the unit moved to Vivigani Strip, on Goodenough Island, where it supported the Australian landings at Lae, and also took part in the suppression of the Japanese stronghold at Rabaul, New Britain.

On 2 October 1943 a G4M 'Betty' was attacked by Flt Lt Ted Marron in A19-142. He put the gunner out of action before Flt Lt Thompson, in A19-137, closed to 200 yards and shot the bomber down into the sea in flames. It was a rare victory for the squadron, although ten days later No 30 Sqn found itself in combat with 18 fighters over Tobera (Rabaul). The unit claimed two probables, although losses were suffered. Another victory came on the 23rd when a patrol spotted an E13A 'Jake' floatplane. Flg Off Drury, in A19-111, slid in behind it, and after four short bursts of fire from 150 yards, the floatplane crashed west of Cape Oxford.

ACE OVER TIMOR

Meanwhile, the second RAAF Beaufighter unit was finding action elsewhere. No 31 Sqn had formed in August 1942, and after work-ups moved in November to Coomalie Creek, south of Darwin, for action over Timor. It was to remain there for two years. The unit's operations were very different from those of No 30 Sqn because average sortie length was about six hours, mostly over the sea. On 17 November No 31 flew its first operational sortie against targets on Timor, but a Beaufighter was lost when it flew into the sea attempting to evade Japanese fighters.

The long flights over the Timor Sea meant that fuel, weather and navigation would be constant challenges for the squadron's crews. On the night of 30 November two Royal Australian Navy corvettes sailed for Timor to extract an Australian Army company. The vessels came under sustained air attack, but the eight Japanese bombers and six fighters were driven off by No 31 for the loss of one Beaufighter. This was followed up in early December with an attack on Penfoei airfield, which caused considerable damage.

During a mission on the 23rd, Sgt Barnett in A19-9 gave the squadron an early Christmas present when he downed a Nakajima Ki-27 'Nate' fighter over Fuiloro to claim the first of No 31 Sqn's 21 aerial victories. Pulling up in a climbing turn after his strafing run

Beaufighter VIC A19-118/EH-W of No 31 Sqn saw only two months' service on operations over Timor from Australia. In July 1943, while being flown by Flg Off B W Gillespie during an attack on a Japanese seaplane base at Taberfane, it was attacked and shot down by A6M2-N 'Rufes' (*via R C B Ashworth*)

Sqn Ldr 'Butch' Gordon of No 31 Sqn was the only RAAF Beaufighter pilot to become an ace in the Pacific theatre. He had spent much of the early war years as an instructor, and was killed in a flying accident on 27 February 1944 (*K MacDonald*)

Sqn Ldr Gordon's first two victims were Ki-45 'Nick' fighters shot down on 9 October 1943 off Selaroe Island. The end of one them is caught here on camera (*RAAF*)

he found himself being attacked head-on. Replying with cannon, he scored hits, and parts of the engine flew off and the 'Nate' went down in flames. The Beaufighter crew then had to evade a second Ki-27 before returning home.

In April 1943 new opposition appeared when the A6M2-N 'Rufe' fighter and reconnaissance floatplanes of the IJN's 934th *Kokutai* moved forward to Taberfane, in the Aru Islands. No 31 Sqn had its first brush with them on the 25th, when two 'Rufes' intercepted a Beaufighter, which was claimed by NAP 3/c Matsunaga as the *Kokutai's* first victory. On 6 May a strafing attack on Taberfane found a line of floatplanes at anchor, and nine were claimed destroyed – Japanese records show that four 'Rufes' and three other floatplanes were lost. More were hit on the water during an attack on 12 June, when Flg Off Forbes also downed an F1M 'Pete', which attempted to intervene. The following month, Sqn Ldr Reginald 'Butch' Gordon arrived as flight commander. He was soon to make his mark.

On 11 August nine Beaufighters, led by Gordon, attacked Taberfane again. They were engaged by three A6M2-Ns and two F1M2s, one of which was damaged by Gordon for his first air combat claim. On 29 August the Beaufighters returned, flight leader Flt Lt Entwhistle spotting three A6M2-Ns taking off. He damaged one and, as he reported, observed a 'Pete' taking off further up the beach. 'I climbed to 500 ft and attacked it', he said, 'closing from 200 yards to 100 yards at "three o'clock", and the "Pete" was observed to nose up in the air and then dive vertically into the sea. Classed destroyed.'

The next raid was not until mid September, when a 'Pete' was claimed shot down. Another epic engagement took place on 9 October when 'Butch' Gordon led an armed reconnaissance by six Beaufighters over Selaroe Island. He was in A19-40/EH-G with his regular navigator, Flt Sgt Ron Jordon, who spotted a Ki-45 'Nick' over the target. Gordon recalled soon afterwards that he was;

'Intercepted by a twin-engined fighter coming from north-west at 800 ft and 235 knots, which fired from 300 yards at "seven o'clock", passing through to "two o'clock". We turned towards the enemy aircraft as it turned south, jettisoned our bombs and followed, closing up to 25 yards before opening fire. The enemy aircraft began to disintegrate, and crashed into the sea from a left-hand stall turn. It had taken slight evasive action to allow his rear gunner to fire, hitting our starboard mainplane and shooting the starboard engine exhaust ring off. The enemy aircraft was destroyed.'

Gordon then continued strafing ground targets, but on his return was attacked by another 'Nick' over Selaroe Island. He said;

'Just on leaving the island, I saw an enemy aircraft flying south, and three minutes later it attacked from "seven o'clock", 200 yards away, closing to 100 yards. It hit our port engine and starboard aileron and passed across, taking up position 400 yards to starboard, then turned across to pursue the formation in front. I opened up both engines and fired from 350 yards and the aircraft started to burn from the port wing root. Still burning, it lost height and crashed into the sea about 15 miles south of Selaroe Island.'

Flg Off McCord also shot down a Ki-21 'Sally' in flames. But, for Gordon the excitement was not yet over. During the long flight home his aircraft suffered an engine failure, resulting in a crash-landing. Soon afterwards, his aggressive leadership was rewarded with a DFC.

During his 9 October 1943 combats, 'Butch' Gordon's Beaufighter was hit, causing damage to an engine, hydraulics and control surfaces. After a two-hour flight back to Australia, he had to crash-land at Livingstone airstrip. Having sustained over 100 cannon shell and bullet holes, A19-40/EH-G was fit only for scrap
(R Jordan via P H T Green)

No 31 Sqn did not attack Taberfane for two months, but returned on 21 November 1943 when six covered a B-25 raid on Maikoor. Near the target two 'Rufes' appeared, one of which was attacked head on by Sqn Ldr Gordon. He shot it down to score his third kill. Gordon reported that he had 'made a "12 o'clock" attack from above on a "Rufe", which, when 100 yards away, half-rolled on its back and attempted to dive away. I did an aileron turn in an attempt to follow it down. The "Rufe" burst into flames and crashed 500 yards off shore'. Another was brought down by Flt Sgt Fergusson in the squadron's last fight with the IJN floatplane fighters – Taberfane was abandoned by the Japanese in early December.

The squadron's main role remained interdicting shipping, and on 16 December eight Beaufighters from Darwin, led by Wg Cdr Mann, attacked a convoy off the north coast of Timor. Gordon, with Flt Sgt Fergusson, engaged four Ki-45 'Nicks' near Lautern. Gordon hit one in the wing root from about 100 yards as it hung in a stall turn, before falling into the sea and breaking up. He turned on a second, knocking pieces off its wings and being credited with a damaged. Gordon later noted;

'They were camouflaged chocolate brown and green with red roundels, and had a rear cupola similar to the "Dinah", with four guns firing from the nose. At that level at 240 kts the Beaufighter could easily pull away.'

By the end of the year No 31 Sqn could claim 18 aircraft shot down and 49 destroyed on the ground, as well as a significant volume of shipping sunk or damaged. The cost, though, was 17 aircraft and crews lost.

On 4 January 1944 No 31 Sqn flew to Drysdale to be briefed for a strike with No 18 Netherlands East Indies Sqn. The Beaufighters were led by Gordon. South of Cape Male, he saw a G4M 'Betty', which dived. This is how he described his fifth, and final, victory, which made him the only RAAF pilot to become a Beaufighter ace in the south-west Pacific;

'When about ten miles couth of Cape Mali, my No 2 reported an enemy aeroplane approaching from the "two o'clock position". I called Flg Off Archer to join me, and did a right-hand climbing turn and commenced a quarter astern lower attack, developing into a stern attack. After one long burst, I saw both engines catch fire. I then did an aileron turn and returned to my original position in the formation. The enemy aeroplane continued to burn, and the starboard wing and other parts flew

off before it went into the sea, where it exploded. After the explosion, petrol burned on the water, with smoke rising several hundred feet.'

Soon afterwards, Gordon received a Bar to his DFC, but on 27 February 1944 he failed to return from an air test in Beaufighter A19-165 at Coomalie. He had taken off to check a faulty propeller, and as he was trying to test it, the 'good' engine's propeller feathered and the aircraft crashed, killing the crew. It was a sad end for a very accomplished pilot.

No 31 Sqn continued its attack missions, but saw little of the enemy in the air. On 16 July, however, Flt Lt J A P Boyd (in A19-189) led a four-ship on a very long-range attack on Maumere, in the Flores Islands. They found two 'Nicks' taking off, and Boyd fired at one, hitting the port engine, while Flt Lt Klugg shot down the second. After attacking the harbour, four more 'Nicks' were seen. Boyd climbed to engage, shooting one down and damaging another. He received an immediate DFC for this action and, after becoming CO later in the year, added a Bar to it.

No 31 Sqn's last action in the north-west area came in November. It then moved to Noemfoor and then Morotai to join No 77 Wing of the 1st Tactical Air Force for action over the Celebes and Halmaheras. Boyd led its first operation to Jolo Islands, just south of the Philippines, on 9 December, but he handed over to Sqn Ldr J C Black on Boxing Day.

Meanwhile, No 30 Sqn had continued operations, latterly from Kiriwina in the Trobriand Islands, in the Solomon Sea, south of New Britain. From there it flew almost exclusively on interdicting enemy coastal shipping.

In April 1944 Flt Lt Ron Rankin, who had achieved eight kills flying Beaufighters with the RAF in the Mediterranean, joined the unit, but he had no opportunity to increase his score. Later in the year, having become a squadron leader, he was awarded a Bar to his DFC. No 30 Sqn received its first locally-built Beaufighter 21 during November, but it did not last long. On the 15th Rankin crash-landed the aircraft at Wama after being hit by Japanese flak over Menado. He left the squadron soon afterwards, the last ace to fly the Beaufighter on operations in the south-west Pacific.

Another successful pilot flying from northern Australia with No 31 Sqn was Flt Lt Pat Boyd. He is seen here at Coomalie with his navigator, Flg Off Fred Anderson, as they pose in front of their Beaufighter VIC. Boyd was flying this aircraft on 6 July 1944 when, during a long-range sortie to the Flores Islands, he shot down a 'Nick' and damaged two more. He received an immediate DFC (*F B Anderson*)

Seen here following his promotion to squadron leader, Pat Boyd gained several rare claims when flying from Australia to add to the solitary victory (a Ju 88) he scored on 29 August 1942 while serving with No 125 Sqn in England (*K MacDonald*)

THE LAST BATTLES

By the beginning of 1945 the Beaufighter had been largely supplanted in the nightfighter role in Europe by the de Havilland Mosquito. The last dedicated nightfighter squadron was also one of the first, No 600 'City of London' Sqn, based at Cesenatico, on the Italian Adriatic coast north of Rimini. Command had recently passed from Wg Cdr Lawrence Styles to Wg Cdr A H Drummond.

Styles had scored his final kill shortly before leaving the unit in late 1944, claiming a Ju 87 on the night of 3/4 October 1944 to become, it is thought, the last pilot to 'make ace' flying a Beaufighter.

Just after Christmas 1944, a number of No 600 Sqn crews had been detached from Cesenatico to Foggia to begin the unit's conversion onto the Mosquito XIX.

By February 1945 the Beaufighter was being withdrawn from the nightfighter role in Italy. Possibly the last in use was No 255 Sqn's final example, X8191/YD-E, seen here about to depart from a snowy Foggia (*No 255 Sqn records*)

Beaufighter VIF V8734/6-M was used by Sqn Ldr George Coleman of No 600 Sqn to shoot down two night-attack Ju 87s over Italy on 20 January 1945. These were the final kills to be scored by an ace flying a Beaufighter (*via OC No 600 Sqn*)

Probably the Beaufighter's last operational task in Europe was to escort the Norwegian Crown Prince home on 12 May 1945. The mission was led by Kiwi Wg Cdr Derek Hammond in RD432/P6-L1, which is the second aircraft in this line-up, seen at Langham on 3 May (*D Marrow*)

Operational patrols continued, but for many months virtually the only Luftwaffe activity seen had been small raids by night-attack Ju 87s. Through the winter even these attacks on the 8th Army's forward positions had become a rarity due to poor weather. However, on the night of 20 January 1945, one of No 600's flight commanders, five-kill ace Sqn Ldr G B S Coleman, was patrolling near the frontline in V8734/6-M when he shot down two Stukas. These were his final claims, and they were also the last air-to-air-combat claims by an ace while flying a Beaufighter. George Coleman's successes were also No 600 Sqn's last victories with the Beaufighter.

After its slow start, No 600 Sqn ended the war as the RAF's top-scoring nightfighter squadron. Most of its 180 aerial victories had been achieved with the Beaufighter.

In Burma, the Beaufighter remained the primary nightfighter type until the summer of 1945, although there was little in the way of 'trade'. Nevertheless, Nos 89 and 176 Sqns both had operational detachments close to the frontline. One was at Cox's Bazaar, which in turn forward-deployed aircraft to Akyab each evening, although standby was maintained at both airfields to counter small-scale Japanese night nuisance raids.

On the evening of 25 March 1945 at a little after 2200 hrs, Flg Offs J I H Forbes and H J Pettridge of No 176 Sqn were scrambled and flew south of Akyab to establish a patrol line, as subsequently recounted in the squadron's record book;

'They were vectored to the west of Ramree Island for 1.5 hours and were finally vectored onto a low-flying bogey. Contact was made at eight

The Beaufighter's final successes in the nightfighter role were achieved over Burma in the spring of 1945. No 176 Sqn maintained detachments at forward strips, like the one at which this Mk VIF is seen running up in preparation for the night's standby (*H Fisher*)

miles. An interception was carried out, which duly proved the bogey to actually be a friendly. A second vector was then given for a bandit at 7500 ft. Contact was made at a distance of four miles and a closing speed of 260 mph.'

The bandit was flying at 5000 ft, with the Beaufighter below. Forbes closed to within 200 ft and identified the bandit from its planview as a Ki-43 'Oscar', so he dropped back to 300 ft, slightly low, and gave it a short burst. Hits were observed all over the fuselage, and a large explosion enveloped the starboard mainplane. The 'Oscar' dropped away to port and Forbes banked 90 degrees to port and gave the Japanese fighter another burst. No hits were observed. The 'Oscar' dropped away under the Beaufighter and faded from the AI tube. The plot also faded from GCI. The squadron record book states;

'The bandit was not seen to crash, but interception took place over the coast and the 'Oscar' may well have gone down into the sea. Claim one destroyed.'

Forbes and Pettridge were flying in KV977/J, and their 'Oscar' plunged into the Cheduba Strait to the west of Ramree Island. It was the last Beaufighter victory in the Far East. And it was Forbes' first, and only, success.

So, in the humidity of the Burma coast, half a world away from the autumnal night skies over the Home Counties where its first victim came down, this was also the Beaufighter's final victim. In the intervening four-and-a-half years around 120 aces had made claims while flying the type. No fewer than 74 of them had reached the magic five to qualify as Beaufighter aces.

APPENDICES

BEAUFIGHTER ACES

Name	Service/ Nationality	Sqn/s	Beaufighter Claims	Total	Theatre/s
J R D Braham	RAF	29/51 OTU/141	19/2/5	29/2/5	UK
J Cunningham	RAF	604	16/2/6	20/3/7	UK
M C Shipard	RAAF	68/89	13/2/2	13/2/2	UK/ME
R C Fumerton	RCAF	406/89	13/-/1	14/-/1	UK/ME
J H Turnbull	RCAF	125/600	12.5/-/-	12.5/-/-	UK/ME
J K Buchanan	RAF	272	10+3sh/-/6.5	10+3sh/-/6.5	ME
A B Downing	RAF	141/600	12/-/-	12/-/-	UK
F D Hughes	RAF	125/600	11.5/-/-	18.5/1/1	UK/ME
C A Crombie	RAAF	25/89/176	11/3/1	11/3/1	UK/ME/FE
J E Willson	RAF	219/153	10/1/1	10/1/1	UK/ME
J A A Read	RAF	604/89/46/108	10/1/-	10/1/-	UK/ME
A D McN Boyd	RAF	600/219	10/-/-	10/-/-	UK/ME
E E Coate	RAAF	236/272/252/227	9.5/-/8	9.5/-/8	UK/ME
C P Green	RAF	600/125	9/2/1	11/3.5/1	UK
A J Hodgkinson	RAF	219	9/1/2	12/1/5	UK
J G Topham	RAF	219	9/1/-	13/1/1	UK
N E Reeves	RAF	89	9/-/2	14/-/2	ME
D W Schmidt	RCAF	236/227	8.5/1/5.5	8.5/1/5.5	UK/ME
M J Mansfeld	Czech	68	8.5/-/2	8+2sh/-/2+2 V1s	UK
M M Davison	RAF	46/89/108	8/1/1	12/1/1+1 V1	ME
R J L Mellersh	RAF	29/600	8/1/-	8/1/-+39 V1	UK/ME
E D Crew	RAF	604	8/-/4	12.5/-/5+21 V1s	UK
A Watson	RAF	272	6+2sh/-/1	6+2sh/-/1	ME
R Rankin	RAAF	236/227/272/30 RAAF	4+4sh/1/-	4+4sh/1/-	UK/ME/FE
R A Chisholm	RAF	604	7/1/1	9/1/1	UK
G B S Coleman	RAF	256/456/89/46/272/600	7/1/1	7/1/1	UK/ME
H G Edwards	RAF	89/108	7/-/2	7/-/2	ME
A M O Pring	RAF	125/89/176	7/-/2	7/-/2	UK/ME/FE
E G Daniel	RAF	89/1435 Flt	7/-/1	7/-/1+4 V1s	ME
M W Kinmonth	RAF	406/89/51 OTU	7/-/1	7/-/1	UK/ME
A W Horne	RAF	219/255/600	7/-/-	7/-/-	UK/ME
W Riley	RAF	252/272	6.5/-/1	9+3sh/1/1	UK/ME
G L Hayton	RAF	89/1435 Flt	6/2/2	6/2/4	ME
T G Pike	RAF	219	6/2/1	6/2/1	UK
M Aitken	RAF	68/46 (det)	6/1/2	14.5/1/3	UK/ME
G Pepper	RAF	29	6/1/-	6/1/-	UK
A J Owen	RAF	600	6/-/2	15/1/3+1 V1	ME
J R A Bailey	RAF	125/600/54 OTU/415 NFS	6/-/1	6/-/2	UK/ME
J H Etherton	RAF	89/176	6/-/1	6/-/3	ME/FE
K G Rayment	RAF	153	6/-/1	6/-/1+1 V1	UK
S W Rees	RAAF	600	6/-/1	6/-/1	ME
B A Bretherton	RAAF	255/5 OTU RAAF	6/-/-	8/-/-	ME
M J Gloster	RAF	456/255	6/-/-	11/-/-	UK/ME
L Stephenson	RAF	141/153	6/-/-	10/-/-	UK/ME

Name	Service/ Nationality	Sqn/s	Beaufighter Claims	Total	Theatre/s
R T Phipps	RAF	272	5.5/1/-	5.5/1/-	ME
J R S Modera	RAF	227	3+3sh/2/2.5	3+3sh/2/2.5	ME
L Bobek	Czech	68	5/2/3	5/2/3	UK
P F Allen	RAF	68/125	5/2/1	5/2/1	UK
H H K Gunnis	RAF	252/603	5/2/1	5/2/1	ME
P E Meagher	RAF	211	5/2/1	10/2/1	FE
P S Kendall	RAF	255	5/1/2	8/1/2	UK/ME
H P Pleasance	RAF	25	5/1/2	5/1/2	UK
D H Greaves	RAF	68/255	5/1/1	9/1/1	UK/ME
H F W Shead	RAF	68/25/89	5/1/-	5/1/-	UK/ME
G A Tuckwell	RAF	272	5/1/-	5/1/-	ME
R L Gordon	RAAF	31 RAAF	5/-/2	5/-/2	FE
R M Mackenzie	RAF	141/409/89/46/227	5/-/2sh	5/-/2sh	ME
P G K Williamson	RAF	153	5/-/1	9/-/1	ME
B R Keele	RAF	604	5/-/1	6/-/1	UK
H S Boardman	RAF	600/153	5/-/1	5/-/1	ME
K I Geddes	RAF	604	5/-/1	5/-/1	UK
A L M Spurgin	RAAF	68/89	5/-/1	5/-/1	UK/ME
L H Styles	RAF	219/153/600	5/-/1	5/-/1	UK/ME
D A Thompson	RAF	600	5/-/1	5/-/1	ME
D White	RAF	CR Flt/39	5/-/1	5/-/1	ME
R T Butler	RAF	108/46	5/-/-	5/-/-	ME
P S Newhouse	RAF	68/600	5/-/-	5/-/-	UK/ME
D S Pain	RAF	68/89	5/-/-	5/-/-	UK/ME
D P Paton	RAF	600	5/-/-	5/-/-	ME
P C W Sage	RAF	89/46	5/-/-	5/-/-	ME
A I Smith	RCAF	252/272	5/-/-	5/-/-	ME
C L Johnson	RAF	227	4.5/-/-	4.5/-/-	ME
D L Cartridge	RAF	248	2+3sh/-/-	2+3sh/-/-	UK/ME
G H Melville-Jackson	RAF	236/272/248	2+3sh/-/-	2+3sh/-/-	UK/ME
J Watters	RAF	272/603	2+6sh/-/0.5	2+6sh/-/0.5	ME
I K S Joll*	RAF	604	4/-/2	4/-/2	UK
D G Morris*	RAF	406	4/-/1	4/-/1	UK
J H Player*	RAF	255	4/-/-	4/-/-	UK/ME
R F Hammond*	RAAF	248	3+1ftl/1/1.5	3+1ftl/1/1.5	UK/ME
D Hayley-Bell*	RAF	604/255/68/96/125	2/-/2	2/1/2	UK
D F W Atcherley*	RAF	25	3?/-/-	3?/-/-	UK
P C Cobley*	RAF	272	2/-/6?	2/-/6?	ME
D H Hammond*	RNZAF	272	1+2sh/1/1 +4sh	1+2sh/1/1+4sh	ME
A R de L Inniss*	RAF	248/39	?+3sh/-/-	?+3sh/-/-	UK/ME

Note

Those pilots with less than five victories are marked thus * in all four tables, and are shown because of their inclusion in Christopher Shores' *Aces High*, and where there may be doubt as to their actual scores

Theatre abbreviations:

UK - United Kingdom and North-West Europe
ME - North Africa, Mediterranean and Italy
FE - Far East and Australia

ACES WITH SOME BEAUFIGHTER CLAIMS

Name	Service/ Nationality	Sqn/s	Beaufighter Claims	Total	Theatre/s
E G Barwell	RAF	125	-/-/1	9/1/1+1 V1	UK
J G Benson	RAF	141	1/-/1	10/-/4+6 V1s	UK
P L Burke	RAF	600	1/-/1	5/1/1+2 V1s	ME
R F H Clerke	RAF	125	2/-/-	4+3sh/2+2sh/-	UK
M H Constable-Maxwell	RAF	604/54 OTU	2/-/1	6.5/4/1	UK
I H Cosby	RAF	141	1/-/1	5.5/-/2+2 V1s	UK
R B Cowper	RAAF	153/89/108	2/-/1	6/-/1+1 V1	ME
N D Cox	RAF	39	4/1/1	4.5/1/1	ME
H W Eliot	RAF	255	2/-/-	8.5/1.5/1	ME
R J Foster	RAF	64/108	4/1/1	9/1/1	UK/ME
G H Goodman	RAF	51 OTU/29/414 NFS	1/-/1	9/-/1	UK
J A M Haddon*	RAF	153	2/-/-	4/-/-	ME
J J Hanus	Czech	600/68/125	4/-/1	4.5/-/1	UK/ME
M J Herrick	RAF	25	1/-/1	6+2sh/-/3	UK
G E Jameson	RNZAF	125	3/-/1	11/-/2	UK
H C Kelsey	RAF	141	4/1/1	9/1/2	UK
A G Lawrence	RCAF	406	4/-/-	5/-/-	UK
J A Leathart	RAF	406/89	1/-/-	7.5/2/3	ME
C A Masterman	RAF	227	2+2sh/-/-	2+4sh/-/-	ME
J O Matthews	RAF	125/51 OTU/414 NFS	-/-/2	9/-/6+5 V1s	UK
C M Miller*	RAF	29	2/-/-	4+2 on gnd/-/-	UK
R A Miller	RAF	89/1435 Flt	4/-/1	7/1/2	ME
W H Miller	RAF	219/125	3/-/-	11/-/-	UK
J S Morton	RAF	219	2/-/-	6+4sh/5/6	UK/ME
K T A O'Sullivan	RAF	255	3/-/1	5/-/- or 4/-/1?	ME
C M Ramsey	RAF	153	2/1/-	7/2/-	ME
N Russell	RAF	272/235	1/-/-	5/-/-	ME/UK
J Singleton	RAF	25	1/-/2	7/-/3	UK
J C Surman	RAF	125/604	1/-/1	5/-/1	UK
R M Trousdale	RAF	409/488	2/-/1	7.5/2/1	UK
D T Tull	RAF	FIU	1/-/-	8/1/-	UK
V B S Verity	RAF	108	1/-/-	8.5/3/4.5	ME
D Welfare	RAF	272	1.5/1/1	7.5/1/3	ME
H E White	RAF	141	3/-/2	12/-/4	UK
C M Wight-Boycott	RAF	219/29	4/-/2	7/-/2+2 V1s	UK
D J Williams	RCAF	406	1/-/-	5.5/-/-	UK
A R Wright	RAF	29	1/-/1	11+3sh/5/7	UK

V1 ACES WITH BEAUFIGHTER CLAIMS

Name	Service/ Nationality	Sqn/s	Beaufighter Claims	Total	Theatre/s
J Berry	RAF	255	3/-/-+59.5 V1s	3/-/-	ME/UK
R N Chudleigh	RAF	153	2/-/-+15 V1s	2/-/-	ME/UK
W J Gough	RAF	68	2/1/-+6 V 1s	2/-/-	UK
D L Ward	RAF	68	3/-/-+12 V1s	1/-/-	UK

ACES WITH NO BEAUFIGHTER CLAIMS

Name	Service/ Nationality	Sqn/s	Total	Theatre/s
J W Allan	RAF	256	14/-/-	UK
H J S Beazley	RAF	89	2+4sh/3.5/2.5	ME
W D David	RAF	89	15+2sh/-/4	ME/FE
R D Doleman	RAF	29	10+2/1/1.5+3 V1s	UK
P W Dunning-White	RAF	409/255	3+2sh/2.5/1	UK
R G Dutton	RAF	141	13+6sh/2/8.5	UK
W F Gibb	RAF	125	5/-/1	UK
R T Goucher	RAF	141/255	5/-/-+2 V1s	UK
W P Green	RAF	AI Flt Drem	14/-/-+13 V1s	UK
R C Haine*	RAF	68/96/54 OTU	3/1/2	UK
P F L Hall	RNZAF	488	8/1/-	UK
D L Hughes	RAF	256	5/-/-	UK
W G Kirkwood*	RCAF	409	4/-/-	UK
R F Martin	RAF	108	5+2sh/-/1	ME
C G C Olive	RAAF	456	5/3/1.5	UK
J A O'Neill*	RAF	176	2/-/-	FE
R J Peacock	RAF	235/227	3+2sh/-/0.5	ME
E M Prchal	Czech	68	4+2sh/-/-	UK
W W Provan	RAF	29	5/-/2	UK
P W Rabone	RAF	256/29/488	9/-/1	UK
F N Robertson	RAF	219/153/96	11.5/3/7	UK
J G Sanders	RAF	255	16/-/-	UK
R D Schulz	RCAF	410	8/-/-	UK
J E J Sing	RAF	153	7.5/3/2.5	UK
G Smythe	RAF	25	5/1/1	UK
M E Staples*	RAF	604	3.5/4/3	UK
B J Thwaites	RAF	604	6/1/2	UK
A Warburton	RAF	69	7/1/6	ME
T D Welsh	RAF	125	6.5/-/1	UK
R G Woodman	RAF	410/96	7/-/1	UK
M H Young	RAF	600	7+6/-/3	ME

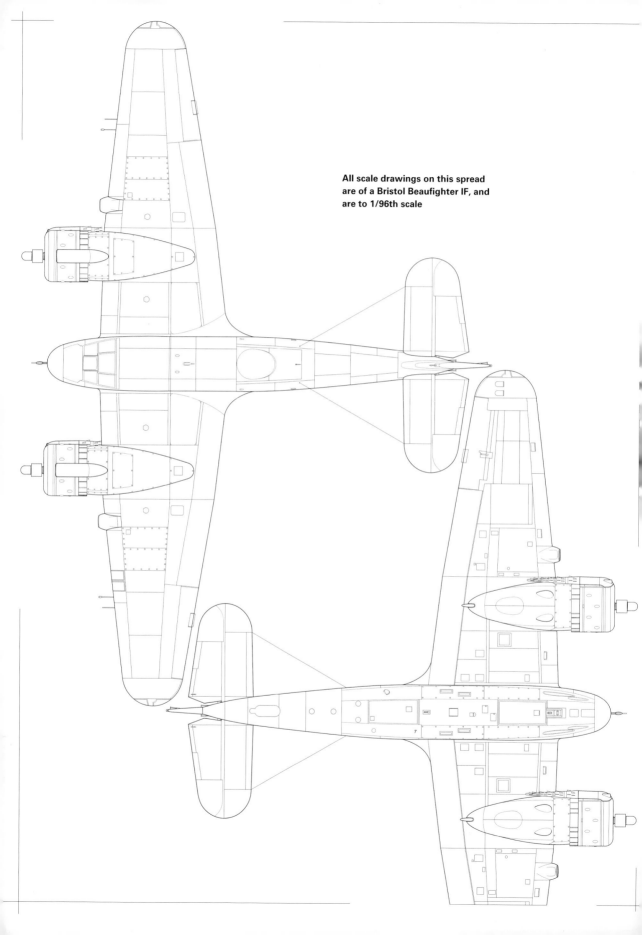

All scale drawings on this spread
are of a Bristol Beaufighter IF, and
are to 1/96th scale

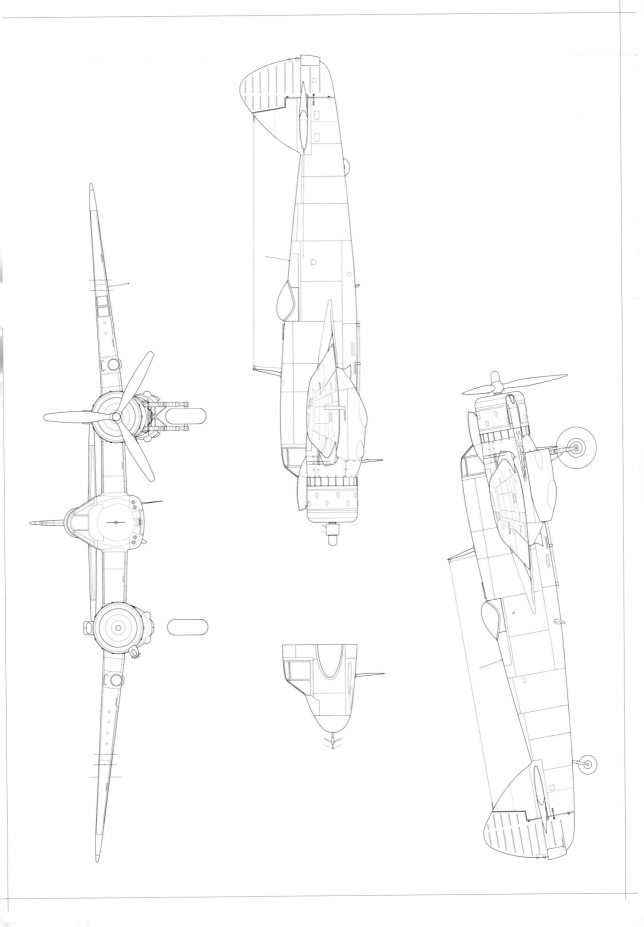

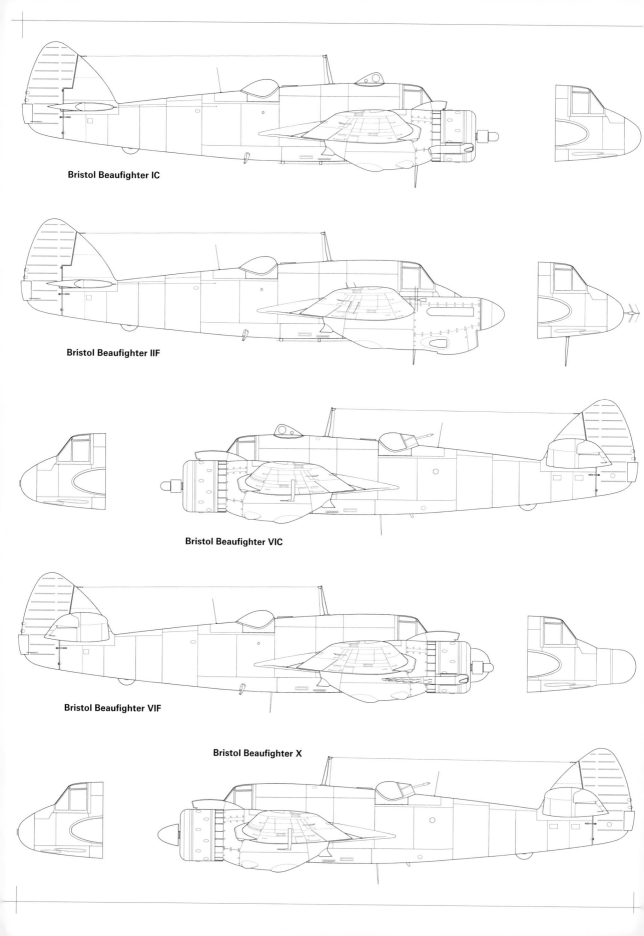

Bristol Beaufighter IC

Bristol Beaufighter IIF

Bristol Beaufighter VIC

Bristol Beaufighter VIF

Bristol Beaufighter X

1

Beaufighter IF R2069/ZK-H of Plt Off M J Herrick, No 25 Sqn, Wittering, March 1941

This aircraft was one of the first delivered to No 25 Sqn, and it retained the engine spinners and day fighter camouflage as late as March 1941, despite being engaged purely on nightfighter duties. Kiwi Plt Off Mike Herrick, who scored three victories with Blenheims, flew the aircraft several times during March and for the last time on 11 May. His only Beaufighter victory was achieved on 22 June, when he shot down a Ju 88 flying R2277. Herrick eventually became an ace while commanding Kittyhawk-equipped No 15 Sqn RNZAF in the South Pacific in 1943. Returning to the UK in January 1944, he joined No 305 'Polish' Sqn as 'B' Flight commander, and flew Mosquito VIs on 'Ranger' sorties until shot down and killed off Aalborg, Denmark, by JG 1 Fw 190 pilot Lt Robert Spreckels on 16 June 1944. Following service with No 25 Sqn, R2069 spent time with Nos 68 and 256 Sqns, before ending up with No 51 OTU. It was lost during a dummy attack on a B-17 whilst still serving with this unit on 24 March 1944, the aircraft crashing near East Maudit, in Northamptonshire.

2

Beaufighter IF V8324/RO-B of Plt Off R J L Mellersh, No 29 Sqn, West Malling, August-September 1942

Plt Off 'Togs' Mellersh joined No 29 Sqn in December 1941 and flew Beaufighters with the unit for almost a year, but Luftwaffe activity had dropped off and he was unable to make any claims. After joining No 600 Sqn in North Africa, he swiftly become an ace. In September 1942 he flew this aircraft, named *Bambi*, with Disney cartoon characters displayed on the nose, several times. Soon afterwards it was repainted in the new grey/green nightfighter camouflage. Passed on to No 51 OTU from No 29 Sqn, V8324 was lost on 17 June 1944 when it dived out of cloud and crashed near Barton-in-the-Clay, in Bedfordshire.

3

Beaufighter VIF ND243/Q of Wt Off R T Butler, No 46 Sqn, Gambut, Libya, September-October 1944

During September 1944 No 46 Sqn sent a detachment to Gambut to co-operate with a Royal Navy fighter direction ship with the intention of intercepting enemy night transport flights in the Aegean area. It met with immediate success, pilot Wt Off Roy Butler and navigator Wt Off R F Graham downing three aircraft in this Beaufighter on the night of 26 September alone. Two nights later, again in ND243, they intercepted and shot down another. Butler became an ace on 1 October when, flying another aircraft, he shot down a He 111. ND243 was named *Kampala Queen*, No 46 Sqn being the 'Uganda' squadron, and it soon displayed five victory symbols under the navigator's cockpit. ND243 was struck off charge on 21 June 1946.

4

Beaufighter IF X7583/WM-E of Wt Off L Bobek, No 68 Sqn, Coltishall, 28 April 1942

This Beaufighter saw lengthy service with the largely Czech-manned No 68 Sqn, arriving on 25 September 1941. It was used by a number of future aces, including Plt Off Miro Mansfeld on 27 November. He flew it occasionally through to March 1942, when it was flown by another future ace, Flg Off Percy Allen. It was at the controls of X7583 that another yet another Czech ace, Flt Sgt Ladislaw Bobek, claimed his first victory when, on the night of 28/29 May with Sgt Kovaric as navigator, he downed a Do 217 off Great Yarmouth after a 20-minute chase. Following its service with No 68 Sqn, the aircraft was passed to No 51 OTU, and it was struck off charge on 21 April 1945.

5

Beaufighter VIF ND211/WM-K of Sqn Ldr M J Mansfeld, No 68 Sqn, Fairwood Common, 14 May 1944

On the night of 14/15 May 1944 Sqn Ldr Miroslav Mansfeld and his navigator, Flg Off Slavomil Janacek, were flying this aircraft when, in a short space of time, they engaged and shot down two Do 217s. These were Mansfeld's final claims against aircraft, taking his total to eight and two shared victories. This made him the war's leading Czech nightfighter pilot. He remained with No 68 Sqn when it was re-equipped with Mosquitos, and he used the de Havilland aircraft to down two V1s in July and October 1944. ND211 was sent from No 68 Sqn to No 54 OTU, and it was written off when an undercarriage leg collapsed on take-off at Charterhall on 28 October 1944.

6

Beaufighter IF X7671/WP-D of Sqn Ldr D S Pain, No 89 Sqn, Abu Sueir, Egypt, 2/3 March 1942

One of No 89 Sqn's original complement of aircraft, X7671 became one of the very few to carry the unit's short-lived WP unit code letters in the spring of 1942. Flying this aircraft near Jebel Mariyut on the night of 2/3 March 1942, flight commander Sqn Ldr Derek Pain and his navigator, Sgt Briggs, shot down a He 111 – the second of five victories all scored on the Beaufighter. During December 1941 X7671 was often flown by future ace Nevil Reeves, although it was actually the regular aircraft of one the squadron's most successful pilots, Flg Off 'Moose' Fumerton RCAF (he made no claims with it). X7671 also served with Nos 46 and 227 Sqns prior to it being struck off charge on 31 August 1944.

7

Beaufighter IF V8447/S of Flg Off M C Shipard, No 89 Sqn, Bu Amud, Egypt, Benina and Castel Benito, Libya, January-March 1943

The most successful RAAF nightfighter pilot, with 13 victories, was Mervyn Shipard. His navigator, Douggie Oxby, became the leading RAF nightfighter navigator with 21 successful engagements. In early 1943 this became the pair's regular aircraft, and it displayed their impressive scoreboard, as well as the name *Slippery Ship II*, the first having been wrecked. Flying the aircraft on patrol over Gambut in the early hours of 17 January 1943, they attacked and shot down two Ju 88s, one of them being L1+RH of LG 1. These were Shipard's last victories, although he also flew this aircraft at the beginning of March to claim a Ju 88 probable to conclude a distinguished combat career. V8447 was written off when its tyre burst on landing and the aircraft swung off the runway, collapsing its undercarriage, at Castel Benito on 3 August 1943.

8
Beaufighter VIF V8748/ZJ-R of Wg Cdr E D Crew, No 96 Sqn, Church Fenton and Drem, August-September 1943
This aircraft joined No 96 Sqn when new, and flew its first patrol on 7 May 1943. Soon afterwards, Wg Cdr Edward Crew, who had 8.5 victories, became the unit CO. On 28 August he first piloted V8748 on operations when, with regular navigator Flg Off Norman Guthrie, he flew a patrol to the Dutch coast. Soon afterwards the squadron sent a detachment to Drem to intercept enemy weather reconnaissance flights, and Crew flew V8748 on one such patrol on 27 September. It was later shipped to India, where it joined No 89 Sqn. The aircraft was struck off charge on 16 August 1945.

9
Beaufighter VIF V8515/VA-S of Flt Lt G E Jameson, No 125 'Newfoundland' Sqn, Fairwood Common, 11/12 February 1943
The leading RNZAF nightfighter pilot was Jamie Jameson, whose first three victories were claimed flying Beaufighters with No 125 Sqn. The last of these was scored with this aircraft on the night of 11/12 February 1943 when he brought down a Do 217 over the Bristol Channel. Jameson became an ace the following year flying Mosquitos, while V8515 probably destroyed a Ju 88 on 13 June whilst being flown by Plt Off K D Vaughan (who later claimed three kills – including two He 219s in Mosquito XXXs in 1945 with No 85 Sqn). V8515 was eventually passed on to No 141 Sqn, and it failed to return from a night intruder mission to Hoya, in Germany, on 18 November 1943.

10
Beaufighter VIF V8694 of Sqn Ldr L H Styles, No 153 Sqn, Maison Blanche, Algeria, 7 June 1943
Laurence Styles had flown nightfighters since early 1941, when he claimed a He 111 damaged during service with No 219 Sqn. But he rose to prominence during 1943 while serving with No 153 Sqn in Algeria and Tunisia when he claimed two victories, and became a flight commander. Styles then moved to No 600 Sqn in Italy, where he became an ace. He first flew this aircraft on 7 June 1943, when he scrambled from Maison Blanche with Flg Off Smith at 2110 hrs, but failed to intercept the enemy raider. V8694 was one of a number of Beaufighters transferred to USAAF control when it established its nightfighter units in the Mediterranean in 1943.

11
Beaufighter VIF ND220 of Sqn Ldr J H Etherton, No 176 Sqn, Minneriya, Ceylon, March-April 1945
One of the few aces to fly Beaufighters in the Far East, John Etherton had claimed six kills with No 89 Sqn in North Africa prior to joining No 176 Sqn in Ceylon in late 1944 as a flight commander. He remained with the unit until April 1945, flying his first operational patrol on 11 December. With the

squadron sending detachments over a wide area, he went on few operations. Etherton flew this aircraft, which displays full South-East Asia Command markings but no aircraft letter, to visit some of the far-flung squadron elements in early 1945. Having previously served with Nos 406 and 68 Sqns, ND220 remained with No 176 Sqn until written off when it swung on take-off and its undercarriage collapsed at Mingaladon on 28 June 1945.

12
Beaufighter X LZ157/M of Wg Cdr P E Meagher, No 211 Sqn, Comilla, Bengal, India, February-May 1944
The most successful Beaufighter pilot in Burma was Pat Meagher, who was credited with five aerial victories and several ground claims. He reached ace status on 15 February 1944 with his first Beaufighter victory. Flying this aircraft over Akyab, Meagher shot down a Ki-43 'Oscar', claiming a second as a probable. His final kills on 28 April were also achieved in this aircraft when, in an epic solo fight, he brought down another 'Oscar' and forced two more to collide. LZ157 was written off on 6 June 1944 when it crash-landed at Chardhuaie after losing an engine on take-off. It was on strength with No 143 Repair & Servicing Unit at the time.

13
Beaufighter IF R2204/FK-J of Plt Off A J Hodgkinson, No 219 Sqn, Tangmere, March-May 1941
In October 1940 No 219 Sqn's Arthur Hodgkinson began the Beaufighter's fighting career when he shot down a Dornier south of London. His next victory did not come until March 1941, when he was flying this aircraft over Hampshire. Hodgkinson shot down another Do 17 to begin an impressive run of success. On 9 May he achieved his fifth victory, also flying R2204, and used it to shoot down four more enemy bombers over the next two months to make this one of the more successful individual Beaufighters of the night *Blitz*. He scored his final Beaufighter victory on 27 July, again while flying this aircraft. Claiming a further three victories flying Mosquito IIs with No 23 Sqn in the Mediterranean in March-April 1943, Hodgkinson was killed on 10 July that same year when his aircraft was shot down whilst supporting the Allied landings on Sicily. Following its frontline service with No 219 Sqn, R2204 was passed on to No 60 OTU and then No 51 OTU. It was written off with the latter unit when it suffered an engine fire in flight and crash-landed at Cranfield on 2 December 1942.

14
Beaufighter VIF V8881/FK-L of Wg Cdr A D McN Boyd, No 219 Sqn, La Sebala, Tunisia, 6/7 September 1943
All of Adrian Boyd's ten victories were scored while flying Beaufighters, the last five in the Mediterranean area when he was CO of No 219 Sqn. His penultimate claim was for a He 111, which he shot down with this aircraft near Bizerta on the night of 6 September 1943. That night four bombers were destroyed, including three by his flight commander, Sqn Ldr W R L Beaumont. Enemy activity was much reduced after this, however, and Boyd's final claim ten days later was also the squadron's last before it returned to the UK in January 1944. The final fate of V8881 remains unknown, as it fails to appear on RAF record cards after January 1944.

15

Beaufighter VIC JL519/P of Flg Off J R S Modera, No 227 Sqn, Edku, Egypt, April 1943

A successful Beaufighter strike pilot in the Mediterranean, Flg Off Raymond Modera regularly flew this aircraft in April 1943, one sortie being an offensive reconnaissance into the Aegean on the 23rd. But on 1 May, while being flown by another successful pilot, Flg Off Tommy Deck, JL519 was hit by flak and force-landed in Turkey, although the crew soon rejoined the squadron. At the end of the month Modera reached ace status when he shared in the destruction of three German aircraft over the Aegean, near Milos.

16

Beaufighter IC T4843/WR-X of Sgt R F Hammond, No 248 Sqn, Ta Kali, Malta, 21 August 1942

Australian Ron Hammond was one of the most successful coastal strike pilots during mid-1942. He made six aerial combat claims, including three destroyed and one flying boat forced to land on the sea. Hammond had been part of the No 248 Sqn detachment sent to Malta to support the vital *Pedestal* convoy in August 1942, and soon afterwards during a strike escort off Greece, while flying this aircraft, he damaged a Ju 88 and destroyed a 'Piaggio' (probably a Fiat BR.20M). Upon returning to the UK, Hammond was killed in action with Fw 190s off the French coast on 1 December 1942. T4843 was shot down by flak during an attack on a German coastal convoy sailing off Trondheim, in Norway, on 28 April 1943. The Beaufighter was still serving with No 248 Sqn at the time.

17

Beaufighter IC T5271/Z of Sqn Ldr D L Cartridge, No 248 Sqn, Talbenny, October 1942

David Cartridge was one of the few 'coastal' fighter pilots to claim five victories while flying from the UK. Flying another aircraft on 13 October 1942, he led a patrol over Biscay and encountered a lone Ju 88, which he shot down in company with fellow successful 'coastal' Beaufighter pilots Flt Lt Melville-Jackson and Sgt R F Hammond. Later in the month Cartridge flew this aircraft on operations without incident. It was also flown in late 1942 by Hammond and another of No 248 Sqn's successful pilots, Flt Lt Aubrey Inniss. T5271 was transferred to No 9 OTU after a lengthy spell with No 248 Sqn, and it was written off on 13 March 1944 when one of its engines cut on an overshoot and it crash-landed near Walton, in Cumberland.

18

Beaufighter IC T3250/PN-A of Flt Lt W Riley, No 252 Sqn, Aldergrove, April 1941

No 252 was the first 'coastal' fighter unit to receive the Beaufighter, one of its pilots being Bill Riley, who had achieved three and one shared victories during 1940 flying Gladiator IIs with No 263 Sqn in Norway and Hurricane Is with No 302 'Polish' Sqn during the Battle of Britain. On 16 April 1941, when on patrol off Scotland, he claimed the squadron's first victory by bringing down a Focke-Wulf Fw 200 Condor. T3250 had been delivered to No 252 Sqn five days prior to this, and Riley flew its first operation – an anti Condor patrol to the west of Ireland – on the 17th. Four days later, with Wt

Off Donaldson as navigator, he flew this aircraft while escorting a convoy heading into Liverpool Bay. Shortly afterwards the squadron moved to North Africa, where Riley was to double his score with No 272 Sqn prior to his death in a mid-air collision with another Beaufighter off Egypt on 16 July 1942. T3250 failed to return from a mission to the Libyan port of Derna on 13 December 1941.

19

Beaufighter VIF X7966/YD-P of Plt Off D H Greaves, No 255 Sqn, Honiley, July-August 1942

Douglas Greaves flew with No 255 Sqn from late 1941, but being in a quiet sector, he found no success. After the squadron received Beaufighter VIFs as replacements for its IIFs, he regularly flew this aircraft on operational patrols with Sgt Milton Robbins in May-June 1942, when it would have displayed Type A and A1 markings. The pair continued to fly occasional patrols in the aircraft through the summer, when it displayed the later type C markings, as depicted here. X7966 was also occasionally flown by the squadron CO, Wg Cdr D A P Kelly. In late 1942 Greaves moved with No 255 Sqn to Algeria, where he swiftly became an ace by downing four He 111s and a Z.1007 between 12/13 December 1942 and 18/19 January 1943. Tour expired, he returned to the UK in April 1943, and following a spell out of the frontline, he joined No 25 Sqn in January 1944 and shot down a further four aircraft in Mosquito XVII/XXXs. X7966 was transferred to No 406 Sqn when No 255 Sqn was transferred to Algeria in late 1942, and it remained with the Canadian unit until it was written off on 11 August 1943 when it had an engine cut on take-off at Valley that caused the fighter to swing violently, collapsing the undercarriage.

20

Beaufighter IC T3317/XK-? of Sqn Ldr A W Fletcher, No 272 Sqn, Luqa, Malta, July 1941

Although he did not gain any aerial victories, No 272 Sqn's Canadian CO, Sqn Ldr A W Fletcher, was still a successful pilot during the early period of Beaufighter operations in the Mediterranean. From the detachment in Malta on 28 July 1941, he led a strafing attack on Borizo airfield near Marsala, Sicily, in T3317. There, he personally destroyed four SM.79s and two CR.42s on the ground. Two days later Fletcher again flew this aircraft, which carried a ? symbol in place of a letter, in a strafing attack on Cagliari airfield, Sardinia, where he destroyed another three SM.79s. Serving exclusively with No 272 Sqn, T3317 was lost in a forced landing 79 miles south of Tmimi on 8 December 1941.

21

Beaufighter IF X7677/TJ-Z of Flg Off E E Coate, No 272 Sqn, Edku, Egypt, July 1942

Unusual in being a nightfighter variant serving with a strike squadron, X7677 was transferred to No 272 Sqn from No 89 Sqn in the summer of 1942. During July it was flown by several future Beaufighter aces, including Australian Flg Off Ern Coate. He first flew it on the 16th as part of the top cover for a mission to intercept Ju 52/3ms, although none were found. It was during this mission that Wg Cdr Bill Riley, who had nine and three shared victories, crashed fatally. Coate scored the first of his ten victories in September, by which time X7677 had been lost (on 20 August) when covering the damaged submarine HMS *Porpoise*.

22

Beaufighter VIF KW103/HU-T of Wg Cdr R C Fumerton, No 406 Sqn RCAF, Exeter, 27 November 1943

'Moose' Fumerton was the war's leading RCAF nightfighter pilot, gaining the first Canadian night victory with No 406 Sqn in September 1941. Posted to the Middle East, he claimed 12 more with No 89 Sqn, before returning to the UK and being given command of his old squadron. The unit was still flying Beaufighters, including KW103, which flew its first sortie with No 406 Sqn on 8 November 1943. Fumerton conducted his first sortie in the aircraft on the 27th, when he flew an ASR patrol. He subsequently performed occasional sorties with KW103, such as a dawn patrol with Plt Off Hider on 4 January 1944. Soon afterwards the squadron began re-equipping with Mosquito IIIs, with which Fumerton gained his 14th, and final, victory on 14/15 May 1944. The final fate of KW103 remains unknown, as it fails to appear on RAF record cards after being posted to the Mediterranean in 1944.

23

Beaufighter IIF T3145/KP-K of Sqn Ldr R M Trousdale, No 409 Sqn RCAF, Coleby Grange, 3 March 1942

Richard Trousdale was a New Zealander who had joined the RAF before the war, and by mid-1941 he had become an ace after seeing action flying Spitfire Is with No 266 Sqn in the Battle of Britain and nightfighter Defiant Is with No 255 Sqn. He joined No 409 Sqn as a flight commander in October 1941 soon after the unit swapped its Defiants for Beaufighter IIFs. Trousdale's first combat with the unit came on 20 October, when he damaged a Dornier. By the beginning of 1942, T3145 was the regular aircraft of the CO, Wg Cdr P Y Davoud, who had claimed the squadron's first victory the previous November. Trousdale only flew it occasionally, the first time being on a night test on 3 March 1942. Soon afterwards he shot down two night bombers for his final successes. Having survived the war, Wg Cdr Trousdale joined the RNZAF in January 1946 but was killed when the Mosquito he was helping to ferry back to New Zealand suffered an engine failure on take-off at RAF Pershore and crashed on 16 May 1947. Following its service with No 409 Sqn, T3145 spent time with No 456 Sqn RAAF, before being relegated to training tasks with Nos 60, 132 and 54 OTUs. The aircraft was written off while serving with the latter unit on 25 September 1943 when it stalled on take-off from Charterhall due to incorrect trimming.

24

Beaufighter IIF T3017/RX-B of Wg Cdr C G C Olive, No 456 Sqn RAAF, Valley, December 1941

Australian Gordon Olive was a pre-war regular who became an ace while flying Spitfires with No 65 Sqn during the Battle of Britain. When the first RAAF nightfighter squadron was formed with Defiants in June 1941, he was given command, and in September the squadron began receiving Beaufighter IIFs – T3017 arrived on the 30th. Olive began flying this particular machine on the evening of 17 December when, with Plt Off Meredith, he flew a patrol over Bardsey Island. He made further interception patrols with it later in the month. Olive

eventually left No 456 Sqn at the end of February 1942, while T3017 remained with the unit until July, when it was passed on to No 54 OTU. The aircraft ended its flying days with No 63 OTU, and was struck off charge on 27 September 1945.

25

Beaufighter IF T4628/BQ-Z of Flt Lt A D McN Boyd, No 600 'City of London' Sqn, Colerne, 16/17 May 1941

Although it was an early recipient of the Beaufighter, No 600 Sqn initially found little action with the type. However, on the evening of 16 May 1941, Archie Boyd and his navigator, Flg Off Glegg, were flying this aircraft when they were vectored onto Ju 88 V4+1R of 7./KG 1 near Honiton, Devon. They duly shot it down to break the squadron's Beaufighter 'duck' and give Boyd the first of his ten kills. The squadron soon began to make up for its slow start, and it eventually became the RAF's leading nightfighter unit with 180 confirmed victories. Aside from its two spells with No 600 Sqn, T4628 also spent time with Nos 248 and 153 Sqns before becoming a non-flying instructional airframe at No 9 OTU on 26 January 1943.

26

Beaufighter VIF V8388/6-Y of Flt Lt J H Turnbull, No 600 'City of London' Sqn, Luqa, Malta, 16/17 July 1943

Canadian John Turnbull was No 600 Sqn's joint top scoring pilot of the war, claiming 12 of his 13 successes in the Mediterranean with the 'City of London' squadron. During July 1943 he shot down no fewer than six Ju 88s, two of them over Sicily on the night of the 16th while flying this aircraft with Sgt Cecil Fowler as navigator. They flew it again two nights later, but made no contact. After his successful tour, Turnbull returned to Canada as an instructor, while V8388 had a long career with No 600 Sqn until it was struck off charge on 31 March 1945 following the squadron's conversion onto the Mosquito XIX.

27

Beaufighter IF T4637/NG-O of Flt Lt R A Chisholm, No 604 'County of Middlesex' Sqn, Middle Wallop, 8/9 July 1941

A pre-war auxiliary pilot who had served with No 604 Sqn since 1930, Roderick Chisholm achieved considerable success as a nightfighter during the *Blitz*, becoming an ace less than a month after his first victory on 13 March 1941. His seventh, and final, Beaufighter success came on 8/9 July 1941 while flying this aircraft when he intercepted a raid heading for the Midlands. Sgt W G Ripley directed him onto a He 111, which was damaged. Soon after they attacked a second, which blew up when hit by Chisholm's burst of close-range fire. An able pilot, he later commanded the elite Fighter Interception Unit and rose to the rank of air commodore. Enjoying almost three years of continuous service with No 604 Sqn, T4637 was withdrawn from use in the spring of 1944 and eventually struck off charge on 2 June 1945.

28

Beaufighter VIF MM856/NG-C of Wg Cdr M H Constable-Maxwell, No 604 'County of Middlesex' Sqn, Scorton, 23 August 1943

Michael Constable-Maxwell was a pre-war pilot who saw action with No 56 Sqn in Hurricane Is during the Battles of

France and Britain. In late 1941 he teamed up with Sgt John Quinton at No 604 Sqn on nightfighter duties, and although failing to score any kills during his first tour with the unit, he added to his 1940 claims flying a Mosquito II as a flight commander with No 264 Sqn in early 1943. In April of that year Constable-Maxwell re-joined No 604 Sqn as CO. On 23 August he and Quinton were flying this aircraft on a daylight patrol over the central North Sea when they encountered a marauding Ju 88, which was promptly shot down for the CO's third success – the first of two on the Beaufighter. Constable-Maxwell became an ace the following year after his unit had converted to Mosquito XIIIs. MM856 was later passed to No 54 OTU, with whom it was written off on 15 December 1944 when it stalled in on approach to Winfield.

29

Beaufighter IF X7750/B of Flt Lt G L Hayton, No 1435 Flt, Luqa, Malta, March 1942

'Gillie' Hayton was a New Zealander who initially saw combat flying Fairey Battles with No 12 Sqn in France in 1939-40. Transferring to day fighters, he briefly served with Nos 19, 266 and 66 Sqns, flying Spitfires, in late 1940 (he claimed two Ju 87s damaged on 14 November). Hayton then joined No 255 Sqn in December 1940, flying Defiants, Hurricanes and Beaufighters with the unit until he was posted to No 89 Sqn in the Middle East in March 1942. A very experienced pilot, he was a natural choice to lead the first Beaufighter nightfighter detachment to Malta within days of his arrival on the squadron. The detachment was duly attached to No 1435 Flt, which had previously been the Malta Night Flying Unit. Flying this aircraft with Plt Off N Josling, Hayton was immediately in action, claiming his first victory on the night of 19 March when he shot down a Fiat BR.20M of 55° *Gruppo*. The detachment was soon reclaimed by No 89 Sqn, with which unit Hayton made his final claims when he shot down two Ju 88s in mid June to become an ace. He had made all his claims over Malta in X7750, which was also used by future aces Flg Off 'Tubby' Daniel to claim his first victory and Flt Lt George Coleman for his second. Hayton was lost when the transport vessel (HMS *Laconia*) he was returning to England on was torpedoed by U-156 off West Africa on 12 September 1942. Although he succeeded in getting into a lifeboat with 50 other survivors, Hayton's craft was not discovered until 20 October, by which time only four of the occupants were still alive – Hayton was not one of them. X7750 was passed onto No 272 Sqn, with whom it was shot down by a C.202 off Cape Granitola, Italy, on 8 May 1943.

30

Beaufighter IC A19-40/EH-G of Sqn Ldr R L Gordon, No 31 Sqn RAAF, Coomalie Creek, Northern Territory, Australia, 9 October 1943

After serving as an instructor, 'Butch' Gordon joined No 31 Sqn as a flight commander in mid-1943 and soon made his mark by leading a number of successful long-range attacks to Timor from Northern Australia. On 9 October he was flying this aircraft with Sgt Ron Jordon, leading a six aircraft attack on Selaroe Island, when they were intercepted by a Ki-45 'Nick', which Gordon destroyed. A second then attacked and damaged the Beaufighter before Gordon was able to send it down in flames and limp back to crash-land at Livingstone strip, in Australia. The aircraft was subsequently scrapped. These were the first of his five victories, which made him the only RAAF pilot to become a Beaufighter ace in the theatre.

BIBLIOGRAPHY

Bennett, Sqn Ldr John, *Fighter Nights*. Banner,1995

Braham, Wg Cdr J R D, *Scramble*. Pan, 1963

Flintham, Vic and Thomas, Andrew, *Combat Codes*. Airlife, 2003

Gillison, Douglas, *RAAF 1939-1942* (Official History). AWM, 1962

Griffin, John and Kostenuk, Samuel, *RCAF Squadron Histories and Aircraft*. Samuel Stevens, 1977

Halley, James, *Squadrons of the RAF and Commonwealth*. Air Britain 1988

Herrington, John, *Australians in the War 1939-45, Series 3 Volume 3*. Halstead Press, 1962

Jefford, Wg Cdr C G, *RAF Squadrons*. Airlife, 1988 and 2001

Kitching, T W, *From Dusk Till Dawn*. FPD, 2001

McAulay, Lex, *Six Aces*. Banner, 1991

Milberry, Larry and Halliday, Hugh, *The RCAF at War 1939-1945*. CANAV, 1990

Nesbit, Roy C, *The Armed Rovers*. Airlife, 1995

Onderwater, Hans, *Gentlemen in Blue*. Leo Cooper, 1997

Parnell, Neville, *Whispering Death*. Reed, 1980

Rawlings, John D R, *Fighter Squadrons of the RAF*. Macdonald, 1969

Rawlings, John D R, *Coastal, Support and Special Squadrons of the RAF*. Janes, 1982

Rawnsley, C F and Wright, Robert, *Night Fighter*. Corgie, 1966

Richards, Denis , *RAF Official History 1939-45, Parts 1 and 2*. HMSO, 1954

Shores, Christopher, *Aces High Vol 2*. Grub St, 1999

Shores, Christopher and Cull, Brian with Maliza, Nicola, *Malta - the Hurricane Years - 1940-41*. Grub St, 1987

Shores, Christopher and Cull, Brian with Maliza, Nicola, *Malta - the Spitfire Year - 1942*. Grub St, 1988

Shores, Christopher and Ring, Hans, *Fighters over the Desert*. Neville Spearman, 1969

Shores, Christopher and Williams, Clive, *Aces High Vol 1*. Grub St, 1994

Shores, Christopher, Ring, Hans and Hess, William, *Fighters over Tunisia*. Neville Spearman, 1974

INDEX

References to illustrations are shown in **bold**. Plates are shown with page and caption locators in brackets.

Aitken, Wg Cdr the Hon Max, DSO 15, 23, 24
Allan, Flg Off J W 'Ian' **26**
Allen, Plt Off (later Flg Off) Percy F **14**, 91
Anderson, Flg Off Fred **80**
Atcherley, Wg Cdr David 'Batchy' 9, 13

Baldwin, Sgt Freddie **68**
Baptiste, Wt Off **68**
Bays, Wt Off Jim **68**
Beaumont, Sqn Ldr W R L 64, 92
Benson, Flg Off 'Ben' 21–22
Bing, Sgt Pat 18, 19, 51
Bobek, Wt Off (later Flg Off) Ladislaw, DFC **14**, **21**, 22, 23, 24, **4**(37, 91)
Boyd, Flt Lt (later Wg Cdr) Adrian D McN **14**(40, 92), **25**(44, 95)
Boyd, Flt Lt (later Wg Cdr) Archie, DFC **15**, 15–16, 20, 63, **64**, 64
Boyd, Flt Lt (later Sqn Ldr) J A P 'Pat', DFC **80**, 80
Braham, Flg Off (later Wg Cdr) 'Bob', DSO* 7, 10–11, **11**, 28, 30, 31
Brandon, Sgt Lewis 21–22
Bristol Beaufighter 6, 7, 9, **46**, 46, **63**, 66, **69**
  Mk I **57**, **58**, 69
  Mk IC **33**, 33, **34**, **16–18**(41, 93), **20**(42, 93), **47**, 47, **48**, **49**, **50**, **52**, 52–53, 76
  RAAF **30**(45, 96), 76, 77–78, **79**, 80
  Mk IF 6, 8
  'R' prefixes **4**, 6, 6, **7**, 7, 8, **10**, 10, 15–16, 20, **33**, **1**(36, 91), **13**(40, 92)
  'T' prefixes **15**, **16**, **25**, **27**(44, 95)
  'V' prefixes 27, 28, **2**(36, 91), **61**
  'X' prefixes **14**, 22, **24**, **4**, **6**(37, 91), **7**(38, 91–92), **21**(42, 93–94), **29**(45, 96), **49**, 50, **51**, **57**
  Mk II 18
  Mk IIF 14, 15, 16, **17**, **18**, 20, 24, **25**, **23**, **24**(43, 95)
  Mk V **19**, 19
  Mk VIC **15**(40, 93), **53**, **56**, **77**, **80**
  Mk VIF 23, **26**, **59**, **60**, **71**, **83**
  'V' prefixes **28**, **29**, 30–31, **31**, **32**, **8–10**(38–39, 92), **14**(40, 92), **26**(44, 95), **59**, **61**, **62**, **64**, **67**, **72**, **81**, **82**
  'X' prefixes **23**, **26**, **19**(42, 93), **71**, **76**, **81**
  'KW' prefixes **31**, **22**(43, 95), **68**, 68
  'MM' prefixes **25**, **30**, **28**(45, 95–96), **66**, 75
  'ND' prefixes **32**, **3**(36, 91), **5**(37, 91), **11**(39, 92), 67–68, **74**
  Mk X **12**(39, 92), **65**, 72, **73**, 74, **82**
Buchanan, Wg Cdr John K **55**, 55, 56
Butler, Wt Off Roy T **3**(36, 91), 67–68, **68**

Cartridge, Sqn Ldr David L 34, 35, **17**(41, 93), **52**, 52
Chisholm, Flt Lt (later Sqn Ldr) Roderick A 'Rory' 7, 11–12, 13, **16**, 17, **27**(44, 95)
Clements, Lt Reg 55, 56
Clerke, Wg Cdr Rupert 29
Coate, Flg Off Ern E, DFC* **21**(42, 93–94), **55**, **57**
Cobley, Flt Lt Peter **55**
Coleman, Flt Lt (later Sqn Ldr) George B S 18, **81**, 82, 95
Constable-Maxwell, Wg Cdr Michael H **30**, **28**(45, 95–96)
Cowper, Flg Off Bob **62**, 62, 63
Cox, Flg Off Neil **65**, 65
Crew, Flg Off (later Wg Cdr) Edward D 12, 17, **22**, 22–23, **31**, **8**(38, 92)
Crombie, Flg Off Charles, DSO 54, **70**, 70
Cunningham, Flt Lt (later Wg Cdr) John, DSO, DFC **4**, **7**, 8, 9, **10**, 10, 12–13, 16, 17, 19, **23**, 23

Daniel, Plt Off (later Flg Off) E G 'Tubby', DFC 50–51, **51**, 95
David, Wg Cdr Dennis **61**, 70–71
Davison, Plt Off Michael 57–58
Davoud, Wg Cdr Paul Y 18, **20**, 20, 94
Deck, Flg Off Tommy **56**, 93
Dixon, Flg Off Laurie 63–64
Downing, Flt Sgt Alwyn 'Barry', DFM 62–63
Duckett, Basil 22–23

Edwards, Flt Lt Henry 51, 53–54, 61
Etherton, Flg Off (later Sqn Ldr) John H **11**(39, 92), 58, 59, **74**, **75**, 75

Fletcher, Sqn Ldr A W **20**(42, 93), **46**, 46, **47**, 47

Forbes, Flg Off J I H 82–83
Fumerton, Flg Off (later Wg Cdr) R C 'Moose' 18–19, **31**, 31, **22**(43, 95), 48, 51, 52, 91

Garlick, Wg Cdr Hugh 34, 51
Gibson, Flt Lt Guy 9, 12, 13
Gillespie, Flg Off B W **77**
Glegg, Flg Off Alex, DFC **15**, 15, 94
Gloster, Plt Off (later Flg Off) Mike 18, 58–59
Gordon, Sqn Ldr Reginald L 'Butch', DFC* **30**(45, 96), **78**, 78–80, **79**
Gosling, Sgt 50–51, 73
Gough, Plt Off J W **24**
Graham, Wt Off R F 67, **68**, 68, 91
Greaves, Plt Off (later Flg Off) Douglas H **23**, **19**(42, 93), 59, 61
Gregory, Flg Off 'Sticks' 28, 29
Gunnis, Plt Off (later Flg Off) Herbert 48, 49–50, **50**, 56–57
Guthrie, Sgt (later Flg Off) Norman 17, 92

Haine, Sqn Ldr Dickie **25**
Hall, Flg Off G A **61**
Hamer, Wt Off Lofty 25
Hammond, Wt Off Dennis **68**
Hammond, Flg Off (later Wg Cdr) Derek H, DFC **49**, **82**
Hammond, Sgt Ron F, DFM 34, 35, **16**(41, 93), **52**, 52–53
Hayley-Bell, Sqn Ldr Dennis **23**, **25**
Hayton, Flt Lt G L 'Gillie', DFC **29**(45, 96), 50, **51**, 51
Heinkel He 111P-2: **4**, 10
Herrick, Plt Off (later Flt Lt) Mike J **6**, 16, **1**(36, 91)
Hodgkinson, Sgt (later Plt Off) Arthur J, DFC 6, 7, 10, 14, **13**(40, 92)
Hughes, Sqn Ldr Desmond 24, 26, 63-64
Hyslop, Plt Off M C **65**

Inniss, Flt Lt Aubrey 34–35, 93
Ivey, Flt Sgt Reginald **50**

Jameson, Flg Off (later Flt Lt) G E 'Jamie' 24–25, **25**, 26, **28**, 28–29, **9**(38, 92), 92
Janacek, Sgt (later Flg Off) Slavomil 20, **32**
Jeffery, 2Lt Rayford 65–66
Johnson, Plt Off Carl 55–56
Johnson, Wt Off H J C 75–76, **76**
Jordon, Flt Sgt Ron 78, 95
Josling, Plt Off (later Flg Off) Norman 50, **51**, 95

Kelsey, Flg Off Howard 29, 30
Kendall, Plt Off (later Flg Off) Philip 60, 63
Kernaghan, Sgt Stan 57, **58**, 58
Kinmonth, Plt Off (later Flg Off) Michael 19, 49, **61**, 61
Kovaric, Wt Off Bohuslav, DFM **21**, 22, 24, 91

Leathart, Wg Cdr J A 'Prof' 58, 61
Lindsay, Capt N H **63**, 63

Mansfeld, Plt Off (later Sqn Ldr) Miroslav J **14**, 20, 22, 31, **32**, **5**(37, 91)
Martin, Flt Lt Dickie 61–62
Masterman, Wg Cdr Cedric 54, **55**, 55, 56
McCord, Flg Off, DFC 79
Mackenzie, Flt Lt (later Sqn Ldr) R M 'Rusty' 49, 57, **58**
Meagher, Wg Cdr Pat E **12**(39, 92), 70, 72, 74–75
Mellersh, Plt Off R J L 'Togs' **27**, **2**(36, 91)
Melville-Jackson, Flt Lt George **34**, **35**, 35, **52**, 52, 53, 93
Miller, Sgt (later Plt Off) R A 'Dusty', DFC 50, 51
Modera, Flg Off J Raymond S 'Red' **15**(40, 93), **56**, 56
Morison, Sqn Ldr R B 75
Morris, Wg Cdr Douglas G 'Zulu', DFC 14, **19**, 19–20
Morton, Sqn Ldr J S 'Black' 29, **64**
Moseby, Wg Cdr W G 'Bill' 59–60, **60**
Muller-Rowland, Sqn Ldr 73–74

O'Hara, Flt Sgt Eric **53**
Olive, Wg Cdr Gordon G C **18**, 18, **24**(43, 95)
O'Neill, Wg Cdr Tony 69, **70**
operations
  Crusader 47
  Harpoon 51
  Husky 63
  Pedestal 34, **52**, 52, 93
  Torch 58
Oxby, Sgt Douglas 'Douggie' 20, **54**, 54, 60, 91

Pain, Flt Lt (later Sqn Ldr) Derek S 16–17, **6**(37, 91), 48, **49**, 54, 55
Parracombe, SS 46
Pettridge, Flg Off H J 82, 83
Phelan, Wt Off Terry **68**
Phillips, Wt Off C T, DFC 69, 70
Phillipson, Sgt J R 8, 9, 51
Pike, Wg Cdr Tom 9, 13–14
Player, Flt Lt (later Sqn Ldr) John 17, 59

Pleasance, Sqn Ldr (later Wg Cdr) Harold 'Flash' 9, 13, 16, 24
Prchal, Flt Sgt Eduard 17–18
Pring, Flt Sgt Maurice, DFM 54, 69–70, **70**, **71**, 71

Quinton, Flt Lt John, GC **30**, 95

Rankin, Flg Off (later Flt Lt) Ron, DFC* 56, **57**, 80
Rawnsley, Sgt (later Flg Off) Jimmy, DFM **4**, 8, 10, 12, 17, **23**, 23
Raybould, Plt Off Eric 15, **24**
Rayment, Plt Off (later Flg Off) Ken 59–60, **60**
Read, Sqn Ldr (later Wg Cdr) J A A 'Jasper' 49, 61, 63
Reeves, Plt Off (later Flg Off) Nevil 51–52, 54, **61**, 91
Reid, Wg Cdr G A **57**
Reynolds, Flt Lt Tim 66
Riley, Flt Lt (later Wg Cdr) Bill **33**, 33–34, **18**(41, 93), 46, **47**, 48, 93
Robbins, Wt Off F Milton 59, 93
Royal Air Force
  Fighter Interception Unit **32**, 32, 33
  No 1435 Flt **29**(45, 96), 50–51
  squadrons
    No 25: **6**, 6, 9, 13, 16, **24**, 24, 25–26, 27, **1**(36, 91)
    No 29: 6, 7, 9, 12, 13, **27**, 27–28, **2**(36, 91)
    No 39: 64–65, **65**
    No 46 'Uganda' **3**(36, 91), 49, **57**, 57–58, **58**, **67**, 67–68, **68**
    No 68: **14**, 14–15, 16–17, 20, 22, 23, 24, 31, **32**, **4**, **5**(37, 91)
    No 89: **6**, **7**(37–38, 91–92), 47, 48, **49**, 49, 50–51, **51**, 53–54, 58, 59, 60–61, **61**, 69, 70–71, 72, 75–76, **76**, 82
    No 96: 24, **25**, 28, 31, **8**(38, 92)
    No 108: 61–62, 63
    No 125 'Newfoundland' 22, 24, **25**, 26, **28**, **9**(38, 92)
    No 141: 13, 21–22, 23, 27, **29**, 29–31
    No 153: 22, **10**(39, 92), **59**, 59–60, **60**
    No 176: **11**(39, 92), 69, 69–70, **71**, 71–73, **72**, **74**, 75, 76, 82–83, **83**
    No 211: **12**(39, 92), 70, 72, **73**, 73–74
    No 219: 6, 7, 9, 10, 13–14, 22, 29, **13**, **14**(40, 92), 63, **64**, 64
    No 227: **15**(40, 93), **53**, 53, 54, 55–56, **56**
    No 235: 33, **34**, 34, 51, 52
    No 248: 34–35, **16**, **17**(41, 93), **52**, 52
    No 252: **33**, 33–34, **18**(41, 93), 46, **47**, **48**, 48, 49, **50**, 55, 56, 57, 58
    No 255: **17**, 17, 19, **23**, 23, **19**(42, 93), 58-59, **59**, 60, 62, **66**, 66, **81**
    No 256: **26**, 27
    No 272: 34, **20**, **21**(42, 93-94), **46**, 46–47, **47**, **48**, 49, 55, 56, **57**, 58
    No 307 'Lwowski' (Polish) **18**, 18, 20
    No 404 (RCAF) 35
    No 406 (RCAF) 14, **18**, 18–20, **19**, 31, 31, **22**(43, 95)
    No 409 (RCAF) **17**, **18**, 20, 20, 26, **23**(43, 95)
    No 410 (RCAF) 22, 23, 26
    No 456 (RAAF) **18**, 18, 21, **24**(43, 95)
    No 488 (RNZAF) 23-24
    No 600 'City of London' 6, 9, **15**, 15–16, 20, **25**, **26**(44, 95), 48, **58**, **62**, 63–64, **81**, 81–82
    No 604 'County of Middlesex' **4**, 6, 7, 8, 9, **10**, 11, 12–13, **16**, 17, 19, 22, 23, **30**, **27**, **28**(44–45, 95–96)
  Royal Australian Air Force, Nos 30 and 31 squadrons **30**(45, 96), 76–80, **77**, **80**

Schmidt, Plt Off (later Flt Lt) Dallas **53**, 53, 55, 56
Shipard, Plt Off (later Flg Off) Mervyn C 20, **7**(38, 91–92), 51, **54**, 54, 60–61, **61**
Singleton, Flg Off Joe 25–26
Smith, Plt Off Albert 48, **57**, 58
Stephenson, Flg Off Leslie **60**, **61**
Styles, Sqn Ldr (later Wg Cdr) Lawrence H **10**(39, 92), **59**, **60**, 81

Topham, Flg Off (later Flt Lt) Johnny 7, 10, **22**, 22
Trousdale, Sqn Ldr (later Wg Cdr) Richard M, DFC 24, **23**(43, 95)
Tull, Flg Off Desmond 31–32, **32**
Turnbull, Flg Off (later Flt Lt) John H 26, **26**(44, 95), **62**
Turzanski, Sgt Boleslaw **20**, 20

United States Army Air Force, 414th, 415th and 417th NFSs **63**, 63, 65–66

Vaughan, Plt Off K D 92
Verity, Flt Lt Victor 61–62

Watson, Sqn Ldr Anthony **55**, 55
White, Flg Off Derek **65**, 65
White, Flg Off Harold 30–31
Wight-Boycott, Wg Cdr Michael, DSO 27–28
Williamson, Flg Off Peter **59**, **60**